For the Love of Teaching

For the Love of Teaching

How Minority Serving Institutions Are Diversifying and Transforming the Profession

Alice Ginsberg
Marybeth Gasman
Andrés Castro Samayoa

TEACHERS COLLEGE PRESS
TEACHERS COLLEGE | COLUMBIA UNIVERSITY
NEW YORK AND LONDON

Published by Teachers College Press,® 1234 Amsterdam Avenue, New York, NY 10027

Copyright © 2023 by Teachers College, Columbia University

Cover art: Chloë Sarah Epstein

All rights reserved. No part of this publication may be reproduced or transmitted in any form or by any means, electronic or mechanical, including photocopy, or any information storage and retrieval system, without permission from the publisher. For reprint permission and other subsidiary rights requests, please contact Teachers College Press, Rights Dept.: tcpressrights@tc.columbia.edu

Library of Congress Cataloging-in-Publication Data is available at loc.gov

ISBN 978-0-8077-6792-4 (paper)
ISBN 978-0-8077-6793-1 (hardcover)
ISBN 978-0-8077-8151-7 (ebook)

Printed on acid-free paper
Manufactured in the United States of America

Contents

Preface: Love and Teaching	ix
Acknowledgments	xi
Introduction: What's Love Got to Do With It?	1
1. Teacher Education and Diversity: Information vs. Transformation	7
History of Diversity and Racial Equity in Teacher Education	7
Access to Higher Education for Students of Color Interested in Teaching	11
"The Overwhelming Presence of Whiteness" in Teacher Education Programs	12
Lack of Program Coherence	16
High Stakes Entry and Certification Exams	18
Recruitment and Retention of Teachers of Color in Hard-to-Staff Schools	19
2. "A Story to Tell": Who Are Minority Serving Institution Teacher Educators and Teacher Candidates?	21
Tulia	23
Jeanne	25
Rafael	26
Alba, Camila, and Elmira	28
Cortez	30
Dean	32

	Kim	33
	Seth	35
3.	**Changing the Narrative: What Does Culturally Relevant Pedagogy Look Like in Action?**	**38**
	What Is Culturally Relevant Pedagogy?	40
	Culturally Relevant Pedagogy and MSIs	42
	A Place of Hope and Healing: Culturally Relevant Pedagogy at Stone Child College	44
	Every Step Forward *Sea Con Paso Firme*: Stories and Images of Teaching in California's Central Valley	49
	"You Can't Sit Behind a Desk": Visibility and Black Role Models at Jackson State University	53
	Culturally Relevant Pedagogy as Community Analysis	58
4.	**"Belonging": Faculty Support and Cohort Models in MSI Teacher Education Programs**	**62**
	Like Family	63
	"Not Just a Number": Personalized and Holistic Faculty Care	64
	Peer Leadership and Support: MSI Cohort Models	67
	My Brother's Keeper: Cohorts and Call Me MISTER at Jackson State University	69
	"They Were Us": Cohorts and the Mini Corps Program at California State University, Fresno	73
5.	**"Homegrown": Teacher Residencies and University-School Partnerships**	**77**
	So, What's Wrong With Student Teaching?	80
	"We Were There from the Beginning": California State University, Fresno's Rural Residency Program	84
	"Their Time in the Classroom Is Just as Important as Mine": New Mexico State University's Blocks Program	88
6.	**Where Wisdom Sits: Teacher Preparation and Community Engagement**	**93**
	Home Visits	94
	Community Service	96

	Parental Education	97
	Field Trips	98
	Inquiry, Action Research, and Advocacy	100
7.	**A Call to Action**	**105**
	Diversify the Teaching Profession	105
	Integrate Culturally Relevant Pedagogy	105
	Expand Student Teaching and Clinical Practice	106
	Recruit Former K–12 Teachers to the Faculty	107
	Promote Cohort Models	107
	Provide Wraparound Candidate Support	107
	Foster Community Engagement	108
	Respect the Teaching Profession	108
	Communicate Messages of Success	108
	Consider the Importance of Love	109

Final Thoughts — 111

Appendix A: The Study — 113

Notes — 117

References — 119

Index — 127

About the Authors — 131

Preface
Love and Teaching

Elmira grew up as the daughter of Latinx migrant workers in Fresno, California, along with her four siblings—three of whom are also teachers today. She did not plan to be a teacher, as much of her learning experience was neither supportive nor positive. In 3rd grade, she still didn't know how to read and struggled for years. She had the unfortunate experience of having an unkind teacher who told her that she was never going to learn and called her "dumb." The sting of harmful interactions with educators who doubted Elmira's abilities left a lasting impact on her self-esteem. Elmira's parents did everything they could to support her despite their lack of English skills. It was a 4th-grade teacher who discovered that Elmira needed extra tutoring, and this supplemental support eventually led to her enrolling in college at California State University, Fresno. It was her experience in college that changed her life, her self-esteem, and her career.

Despite having no desire to be a teacher, and resisting when she was first asked, Elmira joined the California Mini Corps (CMC) pre-service teaching program, which was designed for former migrant students, giving them the opportunity to tutor and serve as role models for current migrant students as part of their teacher preparation. While part of the CMC, Elmira began to see "the beauty of teaching"; she "fell in love with it." The love that she began to feel was the result of encounters she had with a difficult student and a mentor teacher. During her first year in the program, Elmira met a student who was struggling the same way she had struggled in school. Unlike Elmira, however, the student did not have his parents in his life. He lived with an aunt who had five other kids and was also raising six nephews and nieces. In Elmira's words, "Little Joseph was in the same boat as I was when I was younger. He couldn't read, and he struggled, and he was always getting in trouble. Every day he would say 'I hate you. I hate you.'" But one day at the end of the year, he came to Elmira and said, "I love you. You're the best teacher ever." The next day, she changed her major to teaching.

Elmira was also fortunate to work with a teacher in the CMC program who taught her that "giving the students love and care is vital to teaching them the actual subject, because if they don't love their teacher, then they're not going to learn from their teacher." As she recalls, her model teacher "always had snacks in the closet, and he had sweaters, and he had socks." She wondered why he had so much in his classroom closet. Then she realized "it's because he want[ed] his students to feel comfortable." She shared, "Students would often come without sweaters, and he'd take out a sweater." He'd say, 'Here you go. Eat a snack. You look too skinny. Come on. Let's eat.'" Elmira's model teacher told her that if children are not fed and dressed comfortably, they can't learn properly. He made sure she understood that teachers don't always know what is going on at home—those things that stop a child from learning. To compensate for this lack of knowledge, he told Elmira, "You always need to make sure they feel safe and comfy so that they can be happy and be able to learn."

Now that Elmira is a teacher, she uses these same techniques. As she shared, "We all live through different stresses, and we have to remember that even though [children are] tiny and little and sometimes they don't know as much as we do, they're still going through tough times." Elmira discovered through her experience in the CMC program at California State University, Fresno, a Minority Serving Institution, that love must permeate all that teachers do, from interactions with students to the ways they design their classes, to the respect that they show parents and communities. Her story, along with those of others like her, is at the heart of this book.

Acknowledgments

We dedicate this book to Nathaniel St. Pierre, the late president of Stone Child College: He taught us the richness and beauty of teaching with a deep cultural foundation.

Weaving the complex tapestry of lessons from our colleagues across four Minority Serving Institutions (MSIs) has been a deeply communal process. The generosity of time from all participants—teacher candidates, faculty, teacher mentors, institutional representatives, and community members—was matched by their openness and candor during our various conversations through our visits, phone calls, and ongoing correspondence. At each of the four MSIs, we engaged with a group of colleagues whose vision for a more equitable educational profession inspired our resolve to amplify their stories and perspectives through this book.

Offering financial support to each institution was an important component of our research design, and we are deeply grateful for the support provided by the W. K. Kellogg Foundation that not only ensured we could disburse grants to MSIs to further develop their teacher education programs but also provided the necessary resources to gather the students, instructors, and institutional representatives from all institutions at a national convening to learn from the promising insights that emerged from this work.

Sharing these stories with a broader audience was possible thanks to the enthusiastic support of our editor, Brian Ellerbeck, at Teachers College Press. Brian's keen eye and editorial support helped us clarify our message to reach a wider audience interested in learning about MSIs' contributions to teacher education.

Given the breadth and scope of this project, our work was supported by the cadre of outstanding colleagues at the Center for Minority Serving Institutions who partook in various aspects of this project. From the administrative oversight of subgrants across multiple institutions, to supporting the execution and programming of a large national convening, to the minutiae of safely storing the trove of data that served as the backbone for this book, at every step of the process we have been buoyed and inspired by the shared belief in the transformative promise of MSIs' contributions to the broader educational landscape.

I, Alice, would like to thank Marybeth Gasman for including me in this opportunity to engage in groundbreaking and transformative research on teacher education at Minority Serving Institutions. I would also like to thank Andrés Castro Samayoa for his leadership and unique contributions to this body of work. This experience reminds me of how important it is to always be passionate about what you do. I feel extremely lucky to be part of the Center for Minority Serving Institutions and to have had the opportunity to meet and engage with so many amazing teacher educators and candidates across the country. I'd also like to thank my husband, Jason Zisser, along with our children, for always supporting my commitment to equity and social justice while never forgetting about the key ingredient: Love.

I, Marybeth, would like to personally thank my coauthors, Alice and Andrés, for their hard work, deep intellectual thinking, and care for the work that we do. I am also grateful to my daughter, Chloë, for her constant support and inspiration. Chloë is love.

I, Andrés, want to thank Alice and Marybeth for their leadership of this book project. It was an amazing learning experience to work with them on research related to MSIs. I am also indebted to my partner, Jessye, for their love and support.

Introduction
What's Love Got to Do With It?

> I am so blessed to have teaching as my career because we can surely make a difference. I mean, we're not the richest, but we're rich in our values and love. We have lots of love.
>
> —Graduate of the California State University, Fresno teacher education program

In 2014, when we began the journey that we share in this book, we knew quite a bit about Minority Serving Institutions (MSIs) and a good amount about teacher education. However, we did not know a lot about teacher education at MSIs. We knew that most public school teachers of color—still just 14% of the teaching profession—were being prepared at MSIs (Gasman et al., 2017). We knew that many Historically Black Colleges and Universities (HBCUs) were founded as teachers' colleges at a time when aspiring African American teachers were not admitted to Predominantly White Institutions (PWIs), and when African American communities needed dedicated and well-prepared teachers to lift their communities out of poverty (Dilworth, 2012). We knew that Tribal Colleges and Universities (TCUs) were developed in part to ensure that Native Americans could remain on Native lands while furthering their education and preserving their unique history, language, and culture in the face of decades of forced assimilation and colonization (Brayboy & Castagno, 2009). We knew that Hispanic Serving Institutions (HSIs) were on the cutting edge of bilingual education and working with immigrants and English language learners (Nuñez et al., 2010; Sebanc et al., 2009). Likewise, there was evidence to support that Asian American and Native American Pacific Islander Serving Institutions (AANAPISIs) were challenging the "model minority" myth by emphasizing the intersections of race, class, ethnicity, and gender (Hartlep, 2013; Nguyen, 2019).

We also knew that MSIs, in general, use a unique framework for education that has been life changing for many students. Research has underscored the many ways that MSIs are deeply grounded in traditions of belonging, care, support, respect for diversity, and culturally relevant education (Conrad & Gasman, 2017; Gasman & Nguyen, 2019; Gasman et al., 2008), thus creating an inclusive space for students of color who often feel isolated and marginalized at PWIs. We suspected that many of the core strategies that MSIs use to support low-income, first-generation students of color in any discipline—such as summer bridge programs, cohort models, community partnerships, same-race mentorships, holistic advising, small classes, and student-centered faculty—would show up somewhere in their teacher education programs (Conrad & Gasman, 2017).

What we didn't know, however, was the answer to the central questions of our research: What, specifically, distinguishes MSI teacher education programs from those at PWIs? How are MSIs forging new models for teacher education? For example, are they creating new pathways for students who come to teacher education from disadvantaged backgrounds? Are they integrating culturally relevant pedagogy across the curriculum? Are they preparing candidates to identify, understand, and truly address systemic racism and inequities in school settings? To what extent have they been successful in eliminating long-standing barriers for aspiring teachers of color? Most importantly, what can we learn from MSIs about best practices in teacher education for all institutions and for all pathways (traditional and alternative)? This book, based on original research at four MSIs, answers these questions. We share concrete examples from teacher preparation programs at Jackson State University in Jackson, Mississippi (an HBCU); New Mexico State University in Las Cruces, New Mexico (an HSI); California State University, Fresno in Fresno, California (an AANAPISI & HSI); and Stone Child College in Rocky Boy, Montana (a TCU). Profiles of each of these schools can be found in Appendix A.

When we set off to visit these programs in person, we were eager to learn from their approaches to teacher education given what we knew about MSIs. But we were not prepared for how deeply personal, uplifting, moving, and sometimes disturbing the stories that we would hear from the professors, classroom teachers, and teacher candidates would be. We heard stories of incredible courage, resilience, and commitment. These were stories of candidates of color who themselves struggled greatly while in school. Many were told all their lives that they were "stupid" or "slow" and didn't "belong" in school; that they were destined to end up in menial, low-paying jobs; that their families didn't value education; that they needed to be put in segregated "special education" classrooms because they did not speak English fluently; that they would never "catch up" to their White, more privileged peers; that the only role for people of color working in schools was that of a janitor or disciplinarian; that there was simply "no money" for them to attend higher education; or that they were more likely to end up in prison than with an academic degree. In Chapter 2, we share more of these stories, which are also called *testimonios* (an explicitly political act that inspires social justice activism). Other stories are dispersed throughout the book.

These stories are particularly important because many of the candidates with whom we spoke were initially hesitant to aspire to become teachers because their experiences at school were so negative. Many started out on different career paths, including the military, but were drawn back to teaching because they wanted to be part of dismantling educational inequities for the next generation. Others knew right away that they wanted to be teachers precisely because of an academic role model or mentor they had in school who believed in them and supported their academic success and aspirations. Somebody stepped forward and told them, "You are not dumb. You can do this. You can be anything you want." As Petchauer and Mawhinney (2017) found in their research on teacher candidates at MSIs, "Instead of an abstract sense of 'wanting to give back' or (much worse) a sense of guilt, a deep commitment to justice motivated many preservice teachers" (p. 6).

OUR BOOK

In the chapters that follow, we explore how the MSIs in this study approached teacher education, comparing them to more traditional models (as described in Chapter 1), and underscoring systemic and intentional innovations that are changing the landscape of teacher education. As already noted, the personal stories and journeys of MSI teacher education faculty and teacher candidates in Chapter 2 help to frame the obstacles, perseverance, and commitment that it takes to aspire to be a teacher of color in the current landscape of American education. In Chapter 3, we share specific examples of culturally relevant pedagogy, which the MSIs we researched embedded throughout their entire teacher preparation programs, as compared to the more common model of having a course or two on "multicultural education." In Chapter 4, we share findings surrounding how MSI faculty and staff provide candidates with both high expectations and high support, seeking to create a family-like culture through cohort models, strong faculty–student engagement, and holistic and proactive support. In Chapter 5, we offer examples of how the MSIs we researched provided candidates with extensive opportunities for clinical practice through residencies and university–school partnerships. These intensive, site-based models are highly scaffolded to help candidates develop teacher identities and dispositions and to assist them in applying methods to practice. In Chapter 6, we consider ways that these MSIs engaged with local communities, not simply through service learning but also through servant leadership, community-based field trips and observations, and participatory action research. This leads us to the final chapter, A Call to Action, in which we make specific research-based recommendations that we believe have the potential to transform teacher education and, subsequently, fill our schools with teachers committed to equity and social justice.

AN OVERVIEW OF MINORITY SERVING INSTITUTIONS

To realize the power of MSIs, it is important to understand the context of this sector of colleges and universities. MSIs are a subset of higher education that educates nearly 45% of the nation's students of color and 26% of all postsecondary students. There are nearly 800 of them across the country, with sizeable clusters in California, Texas, Florida, and New York. Roughly half of MSIs are community colleges. Although there are multiple federal designations of MSIs,[1] for this book, we explored teacher education programs at four types of MSIs: an HBCU, an HSI, a TCU, and an AANAPISI. Although these four types of institutions are grouped under the nomenclature of MSI, they are quite different in history, make-up, traditions, and place on the higher education landscape. MSIs include 2-year, 4-year, public, private, large, small, religiously affiliated, and sectarian institutions (Castro Samayoa & Gasman, 2019; Conrad & Gasman, 2015; Garcia, 2019; Gasman & Conrad, 2013; Gasman, 2007).

HBCUs and TCUs are institutions that were established with the express purpose of educating African Americans and Native Americans, respectively. Their mission, traditions, and purpose are linked to those students and communities they serve (Conrad & Gasman, 2015). In contrast, HSIs and AANAPISIs are MSIs because of demographic shifts in the country. They used to be majority institutions or PWIs. In many cases, the culture of these institutions has changed to be representative of the student populations that they serve. For example, there are HSIs that are deeply committed to serving Latinx students and boast student bodies that are over 75% Latinx, such as the University of Texas, El Paso (Garcia, 2019). However, given that an institution only needs to enroll a student body that is 25% Latinx, there are also institutions that are on the cusp of serving their Latinx students. These institutions, which account for the majority of MSIs, are the fastest growing segment of MSIs and are incredibly diverse in their make-up. AANAPISIs are like HSIs in that some of them have large Asian American and Pacific Islander (AAPI) populations, such as De Anza Community College in California. However, there are others that only have a small segment of low-income AAPI students and have not been serving them for very long (Conrad & Gasman, 2015).

Although MSIs are quite different across institutional sectors and within each sector, they have characteristics in common. They serve large numbers of low-income students, first-generation students, and students of color. They often have lower graduation and retention rates because they serve students who are less likely to graduate in 6 years. They tend to have fewer institutional resources, to be located near diverse communities, and to be highly tuition-driven, meaning they do not have large endowments and they rely on tuition to sustain the institution (Conrad & Gasman, 2015; Gasman & Conrad, 2013). Despite having fewer resources, MSIs disproportionately graduate low-income students and prepare them for further education, be it transfer from MSI community colleges to 4-year MSIs or other institutions, or preparation for graduate school.

MSIs, overall, have a reputation for providing wrap-around services for their students to bolster their success. They have diverse faculties that tend to believe in the inherent success of their students and communicate this belief to students directly (Castro Samayoa & Gasman, 2019; Conrad & Gasman, 2015; Gasman & Conrad, 2013). MSIs—especially HBCUs and TCUs—also boast a family-like environment that is built around intrusive advising, which means that faculty and staff take the initiative to ensure that students meet their academic and personal obligations (Conrad & Gasman, 2015; Gasman & Esters, forthcoming). These strengths support students overall, and in the case of this book, they support teacher education students who seek to serve communities of color—most often the communities that they were raised in—in rich and meaningful ways.

The chapters that follow tell the stories of MSIs and how they do the important work of molding students into exemplary teachers who embrace culturally relevant teaching, value bilingualism and see it as an asset, provide extensive opportunities for practice, and nurture the desire to give back to the surrounding community.

CHAPTER 1

Teacher Education and Diversity
Information vs. Transformation

> Teacher education for diversity involves much more than the transfer of information from teacher educators to their students. It involves the profound transformation of people and of the worldviews and assumptions that they have carried with them for their entire lives. (Melnick & Zeichner, 1995, p. 14)

The MSIs featured in this book illustrate new institutional methods and models for preparing teachers that embed diversity and equity as core components of quality teacher preparation and teaching. To understand what makes these approaches so innovative and effective, we briefly review current research on and common critiques of teacher education programs at PWIs. It is important to note that many if not most PWIs have as part of their mission statement a commitment to preparing teacher candidates to be advocates for educational equity or social justice. While these intentions have been met with relative degrees of success, our goal here is not to dismiss these efforts or dismantle these programs. Instead, we believe that our research about teacher education programs at MSIs can inform how all teacher education programs incorporate engaging approaches that can lead to a more culturally diverse and culturally proficient teaching profession and help to close the achievement and opportunity gaps for students of color. We begin with a brief history of diversity and racial equity in teacher education.

HISTORY OF DIVERSITY AND RACIAL EQUITY IN TEACHER EDUCATION

It is important to note that debates about preparing teachers to work with students of color, low-income students, and underserved groups are not new. For years, colleges of education have been grappling with how to position issues of race, equity, and social justice within a larger programmatic and institutional framework of teaching. According to Goodwin, "The idea of including cultural diversity training in preservice teacher education programs began gaining currency in the early 1970's" (1997, p. 9). Partially as a response to civil rights activism, school desegregation mandates, and an increasing interest in racial and ethnic studies in education, many teacher education programs added a course or two on multicultural education, began to place their student teachers in more racially diverse schools, and created special pathways for candidates interested in bilingual education or urban education (Goodwin, 1997; Gordon, 2000; Zeichner & Liston, 1990). Many of these early efforts, however, approached racial equity and multicultural education from a melting pot or assimilationist perspective that strove to teach teachers to be colorblind (King, 1991; Milner, 2012; Ullucci & Battey, 2011). As a result, they confused equality (treating all students the same) with equity (increasing opportunities for underserved students and dismantling systemic racism and barriers to achievement). In her review of research on teacher education, Sleeter (2001) found that historically, "White preservice students interpret social change as meaning almost any kind of change except changing structural inequalities, and many regard programs to remedy racial discrimination as discriminatory against Whites" (p. 95). It was also common to frame diversity as "a problem rather than a resource," leading teacher candidates to view students of color from a purely deficit perspective (Melnick & Zeichner, 1995, p. 5).

In the 1990s and early 2000s there was a seismic shift in teacher education programs, curriculum development, teaching, and research on teaching, as the achievement gap for students of color continued to widen and new federal policies such as No Child Left Behind (NCLB) in 2001 required schools to address this gap or risk losing funding and support. Unfortunately, many educators and school leaders interpreted this call to action narrowly, with an almost singular focus on raising test scores for students of color. During this time, however, a growing number of research studies, national reports, and edited volumes about diversity in teacher education laid out roadmaps for more substantive changes in the way teacher candidates were prepared to work with culturally diverse and underserved students (Dilworth, 1992; King et al., 1997). For example, many teacher education programs made more transparent and concerted efforts to diversify the teaching profession to be more reflective of the student population by strategically recruiting candidates of color, to include more coursework on multicultural education, and to offer candidates culturally diverse field placements (Goodwin, 1997; Villages & Lucas, 2007).

While these efforts were a step in the right direction, many of them turned out to be surface level, focused on the efforts of individual teacher education faculty members rather than transformative systemic change in teacher education programs. In the 1990s, most teacher educators and candidates remained White, and schools of education had not undergone the kind of institutional change needed to prepare teachers to work with ethnoracially diverse groups of students and challenge systemic racism in schools. In fact, the impetus to be more conscious of racism in education led to a push-back among more conservative faculty and administrators who considered themselves "gatekeepers for the status quo." As Pang et al. (1997) remarked on their efforts to create a consortium and 2-week professional development session on multicultural education for teacher education faculty at 15 different institutions of higher education:

> We found that most institutions of higher learning are gatekeepers for the status quo and that organizations are slow to change. Issues of equity and culture are complex, and the power structure of colleges and schools is built upon a social hierarchy of exclusion. Although professors of color may be recruited or new books with cultural content added to the bookstore shelves, the power structure remains solidly in place. (p. 55)

The same year, in their assessment of the National Council for Accreditation of Teacher Education's (NCATE's) professional development standards, Melnick and Zeichner came to a similar conclusion: "Despite the rhetoric to the contrary, efforts to reform U.S. teacher education to address cultural diversity are severely hampered by the cultural insularity of the bulk of the education professoriate and the lack of commitment to cultural diversity in teacher education institutions" (1997, p. 33).

Little had changed over a decade later when Ball and Tyson published the most comprehensive collection on the subject, *Studying Diversity in Teacher Education* (2011), wherein they called on scholars to "identify action steps that can advance the research on diversity in teaching and teacher education" (p. 412). In addition to core chapters such as "Preparing Teachers for Diversity in the 21st Century," this collection of groundbreaking essays expanded the dialogue about what "diversity" meant, adding much needed nuance by addressing a wide range of issues within multicultural teacher education, such as teaching LGBTQ students, Black men and literacy, working with students with disabilities, supporting English language learners (ELL), teaching Native American youth, and working in urban classrooms. June Gordon's book *The Color of Teaching* (2000) likewise included separate chapters on African American, Latinx, Native American, and Asian American teachers. She stressed that "Meeting the need for teachers who can understand the complexity of cultures that populate our school yards is essential for both children's success and our collective well-being" (p. 2). Based on original research, these publications, among many others, questioned color-evasive ideologies of teaching and called for teacher educators to help candidates prepare for a wide range of student diversity in an equally wide range of educational contexts, classrooms, and communities.

Nonetheless, there remained a lack of clarity about what specific skills, competencies, and worldviews defined a teacher who would be successful in closing the opportunity gap, engaging students from diverse cultures, and challenging systemic racism in education—three interacting and critical imperatives. For example, in "Diversity and Teacher Education: A Historical Perspective on Research and Policy," Grant and Gibson posed what on the surface may have appeared to be benign questions: "What programs and pathways are successful at educating culturally competent teachers?" and "What distinguishes these programs and pathways?" (2011, p. 50). The answers to both questions were then and continue to be highly politicized and disputed. Even the term "culturally competent teachers" is fraught, as many teacher education faculty members, accrediting agencies, policymakers, and funders make a distinction between general teacher preparation and quality, and success in working with diverse students of color. Chapman (2011) emphasized that "The binary between quality and diversity must be aggressively challenged and dissolved in order for more students to enter the ranks of the teaching profession" (p. 252). In other words, successfully raising the academic engagement and achievement of students of color is not a specialty within teacher education; it is the bar from which all good teachers must be evaluated. Ultimately, despite many efforts to reform teacher education, the same challenges and deficit-based ideologies about students of color in the 1960s and 1970s remained in place in the 21st century, simply recycled in new language. As Ladson-Billings (2005) reflects on diversity and teacher education:

> For some reason, teacher educators have had limited success in promulgating diversity as a value-added factor. Instead, much of our rhetoric, although having the veneer of diversity, is an updated version of the 1960s and 1970s cultural deficit discourse. From their first course in professional education—School and Society or Introduction to Teaching—students begin to hear about the "dangerous" and "extraordinary challenges" of teaching "urban" children. We draw close attention to student lack—"high percentage of free lunch eligible," "at risk," "single parents"—and pay little attention to student strengths—resilience, eagerness, energy, and creativity. (p. 231)

Today, while the U.S. student population in public elementary and secondary schools is over 54% students of color, teachers remain over 75% White (National Center for Education Statistics, 2022). The goals for diversifying the teaching profession and integrating issues of diversity, equity, and inclusion across teacher education have taken on a renewed urgency. The current literature on teacher education is rich with mixed-method research, case studies, testimonials, and calls for action designed to transform teacher education so that cultural diversity and proficiency is integral to the success of any program. While it is beyond the scope of this chapter to cite and explore even a small fraction of this literature, we do summarize and highlight here some of the most common critiques and compelling findings about diversity (or the lack thereof) in teacher education, looking across the entire teacher education pipeline, including (1) access to higher education for students of color interested in teaching; (2) the "overwhelming presence of Whiteness" in teacher education (Sleeter, 2001); (3) lack of program coherence including large gaps between coursework and school-based practice; (4) limited opportunities for candidate exposure to authentic multicultural classrooms and communities, including formative opportunities to practice using culturally relevant pedagogy in diverse settings; (5) high-stakes entry and certification exams that test many qualified candidates of color out of teaching; and (6) problems with the retention of teachers of color as they relate to their preparation. Our purpose for exploring this foundational research is to help set the stage for the chapters that come in which we illuminate disruptive and promising practices at MSIs that can address these issues and provide us with a call for action and new path forward.

ACCESS TO HIGHER EDUCATION FOR STUDENTS OF COLOR INTERESTED IN TEACHING

Americans often forget that as late as the 1960s most African American, Latino, and Native American students were educated in wholly segregated schools funded at rates many times lower than those serving whites and were excluded from many higher education institutions entirely. (Darling-Hammond, 1998, n.p.)

Even after U.S. public schools were legally mandated to desegregate (*Brown v. Board of Education*, 1954) the quality and experience of secondary schooling in the United States remains vastly unequal for most students of color, reflecting what Kozol (2012) called savage inequalities. Schools that have high concentrations of students of color are likely to be situated in poor neighborhoods, to work with vastly smaller budgets and resources, and to have high levels of teacher turnover. Aspiring teachers of color are thus more likely to have attended secondary schools offering minimal college preparation courses, to come from first-generation and low-income backgrounds; to be automatically placed into vocational career tracks; to lack role models, tutors, and counselors who can adequately guide and support them through the college admissions process; and to lack the necessary funding to pay for and attend 4-year institutions (Carver-Thomas, 2018; Center for American Progress, 2017; Duncheon, 2021; Williams & Davis, 2000). In her study of college readiness among first-generation urban high school students, Duncheon (2021) concludes that "poverty, systemic racism, and inequitable resource allocation commingle in urban school contexts to disrupt postsecondary opportunity" (p. 1365). While research also suggests that many prospective teachers of color are committed to working in low-income, underserved, high-needs districts and schools, much like those they came from, the challenges of getting into and paying for higher education can halt these aspirations before they even get in the door (Carver-Thomas, 2018).

Among those students of color who successfully access higher education, research shows that they are less likely to graduate in 4 years, partially because of having to balance schoolwork with part- or full-time employment and because they are subjected to environments that exacerbate feelings of isolation and marginalization. According to Edwards (2019), "Whether they feel as though they do not belong (i.e., imposter syndrome) or they feel as if they must prove they belong (i.e., stereotype threat), some marginalized groups are hyperaware of how they are othered, and this awareness influences how they navigate spaces" (p. 20). As a result, many students of color drop out of college or fail to take advantage of academic, extracurricular, and social opportunities that would support their success in their higher education experience (Conrad & Gasman, 2017).

It should also be noted that pursuing a degree in teaching is not a particularly popular choice for low-income students of color who worry about finding higher paying employment prospects to minimize the impact of student loans and financial debt. According to Carver-Thomas, "Currently, college students of color are less likely to enroll in TPPs (teacher preparation programs) than are White college students, despite an increase in overall college enrollment over the past 2 decades for students of color. The increasing debt burden of college may play a role in declining interest in pursuing education careers" (2018, p. 11). Many students of color also forgo careers in teaching because of pressures from their families to choose a profession with a higher status and/or because their own experiences in school were so negative that they are wary of re-entering those buildings (Dixon & Griffin, 2019). For those students of color who can enter and persist in higher education, and who remain committed to the teaching profession, their experience in teacher education programs comes with another set of challenges, many of which fall under what Sleeter has termed "the overwhelming presence of Whiteness" (Sleeter, 2001).

"THE OVERWHELMING PRESENCE OF WHITENESS" IN TEACHER EDUCATION PROGRAMS

> Preservice teachers of color encounter teacher preparation programs that are marginalizing, isolating, and not culturally affirming. . . . these studies force us to contend with the fact that we are recruiting teachers of color into spaces where they are limited, dehumanized, and alienated from their professional identity and goals. (Jackson and Kohli, 2016, p. 6)

As previously noted, teacher education programs have been trying for decades to adequately address issues of cultural diversity and equity, both in terms of diversifying the candidates in their programs, as well as in successfully preparing these candidates to be culturally proficient teachers with diverse groups of students. Despite these efforts, research has pointed to many ways in which teacher education programs are still steeped in White culture and are designed for primarily White students, including the following: (1) Teacher education faculty are disproportionately White, and many have never worked in multicultural schools and communities or had sustained opportunities to reflect on their own biases and stereotypes about race (Gist et al., 2019). (2) Many teacher education programs still promote false ideologies about meritocracy and education as "the great equalizer" and focus on qualities such as grit and resilience while ignoring systemic racism and inequities that disadvantage students of color (Milner, 2010).

As Gist et al. (2019) suggest, research and policy reports underscore the need to increase racial diversity in the teacher education workforce to be on par with the student demographics; however, we must also address the demographics and prior experiences of teacher education faculty. In fact, teacher education faculty are over 76% White (Marchitello & Trinidad, 2019), a statistic that has changed little over the years (Carter Andrews et al., 2021; Goodwin, 2004). This has huge ramifications for what happens in teacher education programs, including how candidates are recruited, how the curriculum is designed, and how urgently a program works to address critical issues of race and equity (Sleeter, 2017). According to Galman et al. (2010), "It's important that teacher educators have examined their own implicit biases before asking preservice teachers to engage with it" (p. 227). Milner (2008) further underscores that many White faculty members "are not unconcerned people per se—a focus on race just seems irrelevant and inconsequential to them because they do not live a reality that makes race important or of interest to them" (p. 338).

Among those faculty members who do make a conscious effort to design and teach multicultural education courses and to engage candidates in self-reflection on implicit bias and cultural stereotypes, their efforts are often undermined by a lack of institutional commitment to this goal. According to Hsieh and Nguyen (2020): "Many teacher educators of color face institutional expectations to do 'diversity work' without an acknowledgment of the additional time and energy these expectations require, and without institutional support for diversity focused scholarship" (p. 1). Research has also shown that many teacher education faculty—regardless of their race—are hesitant to bring up issues of racism and educational inequity in their courses for fear of making White students uncomfortable, being viewed as overtly political by senior faculty and institutional stakeholders, and/or receiving negative course evaluations. As Galman et al. (2010) found:

> Conversations about race and racism in teacher education contexts often miss the mark because they fail to make clear not only the "fraughtness" of this grappling but also the concept of power, rushing instead down the blind but familiar alley of colorblindness and multiculturalism, both of which protect

white racial knowledge by neutralizing the role of power and reframing race as a sanitized discourse of culture or difference. (p. 227)

All these issues have a ripple effect on the kinds of teacher education courses that are offered and the extent to which they address cultural diversity and systemic racism in schools. For example, even though most colleges of education and teacher education programs now offer at least one course on multicultural education or cultural diversity, the content of these courses continues to reflect "White sensibilities" (Sleeter, 2017, p. 158). Critics note that many multicultural education courses fail to address the underlying, systemic causes of educational racism and inequality, portraying students of color primarily from a deficit or "damage-centered" perspective (Tuck, 2009). These courses focus more on what students of color lack than on the rich cultural resources and experiences they bring with them to the classroom (Cross, 2005; Gist et al., 2019; Tuck, 2009, Yosso, 2005).

A related issue is that many multicultural education courses adopt a "heroes and holidays" approach to understanding culture. In "Supporting Critical Multicultural Teacher Educators," for example, Gorski and Parekh (2020) examined the ideological stances that commonly inform multicultural teacher education course design and concluded that most of these courses emphasize assimilationist perspectives that encourage prospective teachers to "celebrate diversity" but fail to prepare them to "understand or respond to the ways power and inequity are wielded in schools" (p. 266). More specifically, the authors found that only 29% of multicultural teacher education courses in their study reflected a "critical approach" to race. These false, colorblind narratives—that any student can succeed if they just try hard enough—can be extremely disconcerting for teacher candidates who have personally experienced the traumatic effect of systemic racism in the schools and communities where they live and will teach in. According to Gay (2010), "Ideally in the educational process cultural diversity is accepted as a positive attribute and valuable resource in teaching and learning. [However,] it is often seen as a threat and a detriment to be denied, avoided, or eliminated" (p. 146). Gay also warns that: "some prospective teachers may come to see 'awareness' as sufficient preparation for teaching cultural diversity and ethnically diverse students without giving due consideration to changing policies, programs, and practices" (p. 149).

Another issue, previously touched upon here, is that multicultural education courses are typically offered as a one-time or stand-alone course presented as something extra rather than a fundamental lens that must be used across all teacher education. According to Sleeter (2017), "Virtually every program now includes coursework related to racial, cultural, and/or language diversity. But in most programs, that coursework takes the form of one or two separate courses, with the rest of the program giving only minimal attention to race, ethnicity, and culture" (p. 158). This approach is highly problematic not only because it sends the message that deeper work on diversity and equity is a specialty or add-on, but also because these large, singular gateway courses in multicultural education tend to lump all cultures together, thus essentializing the experience of communities of color.

While it is important that teacher education candidates learn about systemic and cross-cutting racism, it is also important that they have a meaningful body of knowledge about different racialized experiences, including the impact of colonization and forced boarding school education of Native Americans, the history of slavery and segregation of African Americans, English language only programs that have plagued and punished Latinx students, and myths associated with the model minority stereotype that don't hold true for all Asian American students. Just being a person of color does not automatically make teacher candidates good teachers for all racial groups. As Gay (2010) notes:

> African Americans may not know much about or spend any quality time with Afro-Caribbeans and recent immigrants from various African countries, or Asian Americans, Latino Americans, or Native Americans. . . . Teacher education programs need to do a much better job than they currently are in helping their students examine the causes and character of the different attitudes and beliefs they hold toward specific ethnic groups and cultures. (p. 144)

In addition, within these racial categories, it is important that teacher education candidates have meaningful opportunities to learn about and examine the intersectional impact of gender, class, sexuality, and other ways in which students of color are stereotyped and discriminated against. One or two multicultural education courses that lump all these experiences together are unlikely to adequately prepare candidates to work in real multicultural classrooms where a single best practice is not going to be enough.

This kind of essentialization of culture is something that MSI teacher education programs are critical of, and regardless of the MSI designation or student population, their teacher education programs intentionally avoid this by infusing multicultural issues across all coursework and practice. Chapter 3 of this book provides concrete examples of how this is accomplished and what impact it has. The danger of retaining a single gateway course on diversity is that many candidates graduate feeling confident that they have learned about culturally relevant teaching in their teacher education programs. However, once in the classroom they are unable to successfully implement it as what they learned was surface level or maintained stereotypical narratives about students of color that did not consider the complexity of cultural identity. For example, persistent narratives about Black men students being aggressive and uncooperative, or stereotypes about immigrant parents not caring about their children's education, remain explicit and implicit in many multicultural education courses. According to a study that Sleeter conducted with 1,275 beginning teachers (2017):

> It appears that although most teachers believed that they knew what culturally responsive pedagogy is, most attributed their students' academic difficulties to factors within the student and family rather than to pedagogical factors under educators' control. What most teachers had learned about culturally responsive pedagogy was not sufficiently potent to disrupt deficit theorizing about students, particularly in schools under pressure to raise student test scores. (pp. 156–157)

Of course, not all multicultural education courses fall prey to these cultural stereotypes, and many teacher educators are extremely intentional and vocal about the need to address systemic racism, but this can lead to another set of problems: candidates receiving conflicting messages and incoherent training.

LACK OF PROGRAM COHERENCE

> In a well-planned program, each course, module, or clinical experience is developed with a conceptualization of how it fits within the vision for teacher preparation based on a common understanding of competent teaching practice. (Hollins & Crockett, 2012, p. 7)

The lack of coherence across and within teacher education programs is cited as one reason why many teacher candidates are unable to successfully implement what they have learned in the classroom. This lack of coherence is centered on three primary areas of teacher education: (1) a lack of collaboration and common pedagogical frameworks among teacher education faculty, liberal arts professors, and school-based clinical supervisors, which fail to provide candidates with a shared and coherent vision of good teaching practices and dispositions; (2) gaps between coursework and clinical practice that impede opportunities for scaffolded, formative, and active reflection on student engagement and achievement; and (3) limited opportunities for candidates to do their clinical practice in authentic multicultural classrooms and communities.

Unlike almost all other academic disciplines where faculty have been trained using core disciplinary theories and frameworks, teacher education is a fragmented experience wherein few professors train to be teacher educators in their graduate work. Moreover, candidates work largely with liberal arts faculty for their content courses and with school of education faculty for their methods coursework. Put simply, faculty come to teacher education with vastly different content knowledge, pedagogical training, and assumptions about teaching and learning (Grant & Gibson, 2011; Villages & Lucas, 2002). According to Assaf et al. (2010), "Having coherence within a program does not necessarily suggest that all teacher educators think the same. Instead, coherence should consider how teacher educators align their beliefs and practices and work together to conceptualize and organize how learning experiences for our diverse student population are carried out" (p. 130).

Problems with lack of coherence are further magnified at the clinical or pre-K–12 school level, where supervising and mentor teachers have little contact with university-based teacher educators and are often isolated, overworked, and unsupported (lacking professional development) themselves. Because faculty spend so little time in pre-K–12 schools, and because school-based teachers are not privy to what goes on in the ivory tower, candidates experience a disjunction between what counts as good teaching in theory and the realities of working in real classrooms and schools where less than ideal conditions impede best practices. Indeed, the scarcity of interaction and common pedagogical frameworks among teacher educators at the pre-K–12 and college levels has led them to be referred to as "disconnected continents" (Bain & Moje, 2012, p. 62).

Much of the onus on changing this dynamic is directed at faculty, who have greater freedom than school-based teachers to reach out. As Pang and Park (2011) suggest, "Experiential learning is essential; faculty must engage in hands-on, real-world learning such as discussing prejudice in schools, visiting urban schools, asking questions of highly effective urban public-school administrators and teachers, and learning a second language" (p. 68). Faculty are not rewarded for this kind of work, however, when it comes to getting tenure and publishing, leading many to keep the schools their candidates practice in at a distance. According to Olson and Buchanan (2017), "For decades it has been recognized that teacher educators work at the intersection of two often conflicting worlds: the world of the university and the world of K–12 schooling" (p. 11).

This issue is directly related to another challenge candidates face, which is large gaps between when they do their coursework and when they engage in student teaching and clinical practice. As Canrinus et al. (2019) underscore, "In strong teacher education programs, courses intersect and build upon each other with the presented ideas and knowledge being interwoven with teacher candidates' work during their field placement" (p. 193). Typically, however, content and methods courses are clustered at the beginning of teacher preparation programs and take place entirely on campus, leaving candidates with few authentic opportunities to connect coursework to practice and to reflect on their classroom experiences in real time (Hollins, 2011).

A key component of preparing teachers to work in diverse school contexts, therefore, is ensuring that their clinical practice and student teaching also takes place in diverse schools and communities. This is not in itself a panacea, however. Candidates need to see culturally responsive teaching modeled for them in real classrooms by their program faculty and mentor teachers. As Gist et al. (2019) underscore about preservice teachers [PSTs]:

> Culturally responsive clinical experiences must extend beyond simply placing PSTs in settings with students of different backgrounds. PSTs, regardless of race, must see effective culturally responsive practice in action within a real-world setting. Culturally responsive clinical experiences begin with strategic partnerships with community members, school districts, and teachers who are invested in culturally responsive pedagogy and are willing to support such aims. (p. 18)

While many alternative route teacher education programs have attempted to solve this problem by putting candidates in charge of classrooms at the start of their preparation, research suggests that what we really need is to develop nonhierarchical communities of practice where candidates receive formative, scaffolded, and reflective opportunities to move between coursework and practice, jointly supported and assessed by university faculty, clinical supervisors, and practicing teachers (Patton & Parker, 2017). It is also important that community members and organizations are brought into these communities of practice. As Gist et al. (2019) note, "Central to the notion of culturally responsive teaching is the belief that teachers must take time to learn about their students' lives outside of school, the communities in which they live, their perceptions of school, and their connections to school knowledge" (p. 6). Community engagement and community service is one of the hallmarks of MSI teacher education programs and a large part of the MSI ethos (Conrad & Gasman, 2017). All these issues are discussed in depth in Chapters 5 and 6.

It is important to note, however, that even when teacher education programs integrate cultural diversity across their programs, these are not necessarily the competencies that lead candidates to successfully become teachers. High stakes entry and certification exams remain a persistent barrier for candidates of color.

HIGH STAKES ENTRY AND CERTIFICATION EXAMS

Currently, to successfully enroll in teacher education programs and to gain the necessary certification to teach, candidates are required to pass several high-stakes exams such as the PRAXIS. There is a significant body of research that shows that teachers of color are much less likely to pass these exams, which has huge ramifications for diversifying the teaching profession (Petchauer, 2018). The reasons why teachers of color disproportionately fail these exams are becoming clearer and clearer, and in many ways echo the same reasons why students of color have trouble enrolling and succeeding in higher education in general. These exams typically measure a candidate's literacy and math skills. The need for future teachers to be fluent in these subjects is not at issue. However, as already noted, many candidates of color come from low-income, poor quality, and under-resourced secondary schools that lack the academic vigor of schools in more middle-to-upper income communities. As a result, these candidates may need more opportunities for tutoring and extracurricular study sessions to get up to speed. While important, lack of preparation is not the only reason why candidates of color do not pass these exams. As Petchauer (2018) has found in ongoing studies of candidates' experience with these exams, other major impediments include the cost of the exam, exam sites that are not convenient or hospitable to candidates of color, stress related to stereotype threat and negative messages from other students of color who failed the exams, as well as culturally biased questions.

Given that these tests are not going away anytime soon, it is still important to question whether they are the only and/or most relevant measures of what makes for a successful teacher. We need assessments that measure competencies such as increasing student engagement, using culturally relevant curricula and pedagogy, holding expectations for all students, challenging stereotypes and deficit models of students of color, increasing parent and community engagement, using personalized and differentiated instruction, and advocating for educational equity in areas such as student tracking and discipline. These skills and dispositions are not just important for teachers of color. All teachers should have to demonstrate these competencies. Many of these important skills cannot be adequately assessed in a test and will require alternative measures such as observing student teaching (live and/or on video), portfolios, and self-reflections. Such alternative measures would no doubt provide us with a much more nuanced understanding of what constitutes good teaching in general and creating positive and meaningful educational experiences for students of color specifically. However, if we cannot recruit and retain teachers in hard-to-staff schools, it will be irrelevant as to whether they are certified to teach there.

RECRUITMENT AND RETENTION OF TEACHERS OF COLOR IN HARD-TO-STAFF SCHOOLS

There is a growing body of research on what happens to teacher candidates of color once they pass their final exams and become certified to teach. Unfortunately, much of this research concludes that the pipeline is extremely leaky, and teachers of color leave the profession at much higher rates than White teachers (Achinstein et al., 2010; Ingersoll, 2001; Jackson and Kohli, 2016). The reasons for this are complex but not completely surprising: (1) teachers of color face racism and stereotyping, often being labeled affirmative action hires; (2) teachers of color are likewise pigeonholed as role models and disciplinarians for students of color, with many colleagues neglecting to recognize their intellectual prowess and teaching skills; (3) teachers of color are more likely to work in hard-to-staff schools and burn out much more quickly due to lack of resources, large class sizes, and heavy teaching loads;[1] (4) teachers of color are frustrated by their lack of autonomy and ability to be advocates for students of color; (5) teachers of color experience praxis shock when they realize that their teacher education programs did not adequately prepare them for the realities of teaching in high-needs schools; (6) teachers of color feel especially responsible for the success of students of color and end up with a burden or invisible tax that is unsustainable; and (7) teachers of color lack mentors, role models, and professional development opportunities that would help them to grow and face adversity (Kohli, 2018).

While this book does not follow teacher candidates from MSI preparation programs into the profession, our research does suggest that the kinds of preparation teachers receive at MSIs are intentionally designed to address many of these issues. In addition to providing candidates with more time and guided practice in authentic school and community settings, which reduce praxis shock and allow candidates to enter teaching with a support network in place, many MSIs stay in close contact with their alumni and provide a family-like environment that supports them throughout their careers.

Herein we examine several reasons why traditional teacher education programs have not been particularly successful at shifting the center of gravity to attract, retain, engage, support, and, ultimately, graduate larger numbers of diverse candidates and especially candidates of color. Such problems with the traditional teacher pipeline, combined with an immediate need for more teachers in underserved school districts with high proportions of low-income students of color, have led to the creation of many alternative certification routes. While there are many pros and cons to these alternative routes, few address the issues raised in this chapter. Moreover, the fact remains that traditional teacher education programs at colleges and universities still have an outsized influence on the future of the teaching profession, and with that influence comes an obligation to address and rectify the issues cited previously.

A better understanding of these issues lays the groundwork to answer the central questions of this book: What are teacher education programs at MSIs doing differently? What is the impact on teacher educators and teacher candidates of color who are engaged in these programs? And how can these new models be used across all teacher education programs to ensure educational equity and justice? As Ball and Tyson (2011) suggest, "The challenge remains for us to move beyond intuitive notions of what diversity means for teaching and teacher education toward more research-based approaches to innovation and improvements to the field"(p. 405).

CHAPTER 2

"A Story to Tell"
Who Are Minority Serving Institution Teacher Educators and Teacher Candidates?

> Each faculty member does have a story to tell, just like our students.
> —Nathaniel St. Pierre, former president, Stone Child College

Before looking any further at the uniqueness and impact of MSI teacher education programs, it is important to ask: Who are the people behind these programs? What are their stories? These stories are important for many reasons. In support of nationwide efforts to diversify the teaching profession, a great deal of research has been conducted about how to attract more candidates of color to be teachers. This research includes trying to better understand why candidates of color choose (or reject) teaching as career, and what factors influence whether they persist in the profession (Achinstein et al., 2010; Carter-Andrews et al., 2021; Gist, 2016; Gordon, 2000; Kohli, 2018; Petchauer & Mawhinney 2017).

Research suggests that one of the primary reasons that people of color decide to become teachers is a commitment to changing discriminatory practices in schools, so education is more engaging, culturally relevant, supportive, and equitable. At the same time, many people of color are hesitant to pursue teaching because their own experiences in school were so negative and even in some cases traumatizing. In his foreword to Gordon's (2000) *The Color Teaching*, for example, Ogbu notes that "Minorities develop an image of the teaching profession from their own experiences with the educational system.... A crucial factor in developing a positive or negative image of the teaching profession is an individual's or group's historical experiences with public schooling" (p. vii). Gordon (2000) concurs, adding that it is not just a candidate's individual experiences in school that influence their decision to enroll in teacher education, it is also the perception of education in their families and communities. According to Gordon, "The choice to enter a profession, any profession, is influenced long before college by the perceptions and attitudes held within the families, communities and schools from which students emerge" (p. 2). Gordon continues, noting,

"A more thorough understanding of the reasons why individuals of color do not choose the teaching profession should result in policies and programs designed to attract more students of color to the field" (p. 3). Noting challenges due to school desegregation, higher education elitism, racism, poverty, and urban decay (p. 3), Gordon concludes that "One of the major educational concerns of our lifetime is the search for qualified and caring teachers for low-income immigrant and minority children who have become the majority population in American schools" (p. 3).

We know from our research that MSIs are, in fact, successfully attracting and retaining candidates of color in their teacher education programs. Even though national estimates indicate that only 14% of all public school teachers received their degrees from an MSI, the impact of MSIs in the teacher education landscape rapidly shifts when we disaggregate these estimates by ethnoracial groups. Over 38% of all Black public school educators received their degrees from MSIs. Similarly, 48% of all Latinx, 31% of all Pacific Islander, and 1 in 5 of all Asian and American Indian teachers trained at MSIs (Gasman et al., 2017, p. 12). These patterns are consistent with the sizeable representation of faculty of color at MSIs, given that a majority of all postsecondary faculty of color are at MSIs (Castro Samayoa & Gasman, 2019).

Throughout this book, we explain in detail some of the strategic ways that MSIs achieve this success. In this chapter, we pause to share—and pay respect to—some of the personal *testimonios* or narratives of the teacher educators and candidates with whom we met. While these stories are inspiring testaments to human resilience, they are also at times indicative of why the teaching profession remains over 75% White.

From the time they were very young, most of the candidates and many of the teacher educators we spoke to struggled with issues such as housing and food insecurity, deportation, language barriers, deficit stereotyping, and of course, outright racism. Many dropped out of high school several times before persisting and going on to higher education, often the first in their family to do so. Once they got to college, they shared that they had few family members or peers to guide them or to rely on. Most worked full-time while in school and/or had younger siblings to care for. Many were older students, including student parents who were coming back to school after significant gaps and students leaving the military. Many of the teacher educators and candidates we spoke with also shared their family's expectations that they should be working, not going to college, and certainly not going into debt for a profession that is low-paying and has little prestige.

While they shared many of these life experiences, we also found some stark differences as we talked to candidates from the four institutions in our study. More specifically, migrant candidates from California State University, Fresno emphasized how they were primed from an early age to join their parents working in the fields, moved several times a year to follow the crops, and were frequently bullied in school. Tribal teacher education candidates from Stone Child College focused on how formal education was a stark reminder of years of colonization and forced assimilation that practically destroyed their communities and wiped out their native languages and culture. Black male teacher candidates at Jackson State University fought both racial and gender stereotypes, as teaching was viewed as a low-status profession primarily comprised of women. Many of the candidates at Jackson State had never even had a Black man as a teacher before aspiring to become one. At New Mexico State University (NMSU), candidates pursuing bilingual teaching certifications told us of their own longstanding fear of speaking Spanish in school as children, where they were heavily stigmatized and penalized for being English language learners.

Likewise, for many MSI teacher education faculty, the path to college, much less to the professoriate, was invisible at first. Lacking role models and family members who completed college, coming from under-resourced and poor-quality secondary schools, working full-time while in school, caring for extended family members, and struggling to find the funds to pay for higher education all threatened to impede the success of many of the teacher educators with whom we spoke. Getting their associate's or bachelor's degree was already a huge accomplishment; now they were looking at years of schooling and additional financial debt to get their doctorates. Accompanying feelings of impostor syndrome are best summed up by the teacher educator who told us, "I was hired as a college assistant professor, by accident I think." We begin with her story.

TULIA

When we visited New Mexico State University, Las Cruces, one of the first people we met with was Tulia, who was then starting her first year as the director of elementary education. Right away, Tulia told us that she was hired as a professor "by accident I think." Although Tulia was the fifth generation in her family to be born and raised in Las Cruces, New Mexico, she confided, "My story is somewhat different." According to Tulia, even though she grew up in a home where Spanish was always spoken, "Speaking Spanish at school was not a safe thing to do." At an early age she learned to only hang out with and have friends who spoke English. Tulia also told us that she grew up in a home where money was lacking. In high school she never thought of going to college, further noting that "There was no support at any level for me to know what classes to take. I barely passed algebra. I had friends who were taking trigonometry and calculus and I didn't know what any of that meant."

While Tulia was learning shorthand and typing, preparing to become a secretary or bookkeeper, Tulia's sister encouraged her to consider going to college and helped her navigate the college admissions process. According to

Tulia, "My parents didn't know what that meant." While she eventually got accepted into college, she shared that "I flunked out, as all 18-year-olds do, I guess. Because I didn't know how to negotiate college. I didn't know what that meant. I thought you could just stop going to school. I didn't realize that the Fs would follow you for the next 20 years." After getting married at 24 and having a baby soon after, Tulia realized that "If anything happened, I couldn't earn enough money to take care of us. A secretary or bookkeeper would not make that much money, so I came back to school." She explained rather bluntly, "People become teachers to change the world. You hear that a lot, they want to help students and change the world. I became a teacher because I would have the same vacation as my children. I had no political, social justice equity aspirations, I just wanted a job, and that just seemed like a good thing to do."

According to Tulia, however, when she came back to school the second time, the faculty was quite different—much more diverse. She started taking early childhood education classes and realized that was the field that she wanted to work in. Two years after graduating and working in local schools, Tulia decided to go back and get her master's degree. It was then that Tulia was first introduced to what she calls "critical pedagogy." She recalls that "All I wanted was the recipe of how to keep five-year-olds quiet, because I was a kindergarten teacher. What happened was I learned that I had spent 30 years passing as White, not even knowing what that privilege meant, because I was light skinned. After I was married, my last name [changed]. When I would tell people that I was Mexican and [they'd hear my married name], they'd be like, really? I realized that it was a disease, I never knew that having been born and raised here. Anyway, that's when being a teacher meant something different for me."

The school district paid for Tulia to get her bilingual endorsement, and she legally became a bilingual teacher, something she was already doing informally with her students given that she was Mexican and knew Spanish. Some years later she was offered a fellowship to start work on her doctorate, which she was working to finish when we met with her. Tulia shared that even though she didn't have her doctorate yet, NMSU needed an assistant director of elementary education. She applied and was hired. One of the first changes she has initiated for the program is that every student going through the elementary education program is now going to come out with a bilingual endorsement or a teaching English as a second language (TESOL) endorsement. According to Tulia, "I think everybody should know second language acquisition and how to work with English learners. Yeah, I think that's a must." Her story represents a long journey from hanging out only with kids who spoke English, because speaking Spanish "wasn't safe," and flunking out of college while unconsciously passing as White, to ensuring that one day all students will have trained culturally and linguistically responsive teachers.

JEANNE

Jeanne was a senior at NMSU when we met with her. She was in the bilingual program with an endorsement in TESOL and math. Like Tulia, she was also born and raised in Las Cruces. Unlike Tulia, however, she became interested in teaching as a young child. She liked "playing with [her] little brothers and being the teacher." According to Jeanne, "I always envisioned myself being a teacher growing up. I always told my parents I wanted to be a teacher, but then I was like 'oh teachers don't get paid really well' so I changed my mind." Admitting that her "heart was always in teaching," Jeanne joined a pre-teaching program at her local high school, which eventually led to her enrolling in the elementary education program at NMSU.

But it was not a smooth transition for her. When Jeanne's father got deported to Mexico, she had to stay in New Mexico to help her mom. According to Jeanne, "My father is in Mexico now. I get to see him every six months. It's been a struggle. So that's what has kind of kept me here because I had offers to go to other places, and I wish I could have had the opportunity to." Jeanne also shared that as the oldest of five kids with a mom who works full-time, she had to do a lot of tutoring for her younger siblings. When asked whether this was hard for her, she replied: "I guess I'm just used to it. Ever since I was in high school, I've worked two jobs. I'm 22. I think I just actually grew up a little bit faster. I guess I've learned how to balance things out because I had two jobs throughout my whole education here at NMSU. Basically, I work full time."

Acknowledging that her work schedule and family responsibilities kept her away from doing leadership activities while in college, Jeanne added optimistically, "But I'm here and I'm going to graduate. I'm ready." Surprisingly, even though Jeanne is preparing to get certified in math instruction, she herself had "bad experiences" with math in high school, noting that she received very little support from her teacher, and she was one of the only students of color in the class. Jeanne does, however, recall several other teachers who served as role models for her, including a bilingual teacher she had in elementary school: "She influenced me a lot. I was a very shy kid in school. I guess she saw my strength and helped me a lot."

Jeanne wants to do the same for younger Latinx students: "I want to help a lot of the kids that came from my background, because I had a hard background. Especially in this area you see a lot of immigrants and bilingual kids. It's hard right now. A lot of kids right now in my school their parents are facing deportation, or they spend their weekends in Mexico. I know where they're coming from." Jeanne's long-term goal is getting her PhD and becoming a professor of teacher education, sharing that "As a Hispanic student it's just something I really want to do."

RAFAEL

Rafael is a coordinator of University Migrant Services at California State University, Fresno, where he also oversees coordinating efforts with programs such as the Migrant Education K–12 programs and the California Mini Corps (CMC) Program. Now in his 28th year at California State University, Fresno State, Rafael describes his role working with future students: "My task is number one to provide access to them, open the door so that they can apply to the university or better yet prepare for the university in a timely manner." Rafael helps prospective students with their applications and to receive financial support. Most of the students he works with—up to 40%—are undocumented, and many come to the United States on their own, without their parents. He noted that while a lot of students are bilingual, Spanish is still their primary language. This experience is something Rafael himself can relate to. As he shared, "We migrated from Mexico. I came here to work. I did go to high school, but I learned that in high school I got put in the back of the room, so I dropped out."

Rafael recalls that "The Migrant Program didn't give up on me. They came to visit me at home and asked my parents why don't you send Rafael to school? My father in all his wisdom just told them 'Why don't you ask him?'" Rafael remembers that when they asked why he didn't want to go to school, he replied: "What do you want me in school for? I don't want to go to school if I'm going to be sitting in the back of the room. I can do better things with my time than sitting in the back of the room. I can go to the fields, and I can make some money to help my family. I don't need to waste my time going back to school like that." Rafael continued, "So then the recruiter asked me a critical question. What is it going to take for me to take you back to school? On the spur of the moment I said, 'Well, give me a tutor and I'll go back.' And he did. He gave me a tutor. Now I've got no excuses."

Rafael shared that when he went back to school he got a personal tutor, also from a migrant background, whom he saw as "a person who would pay attention to my needs." But even then, it was not easy for him "because of the bullying." According to Rafael, "Bullying was never addressed by the migrant program. I just survived on my own." When we asked who bullied him, Rafael replied, "Everybody." He was bullied for several reasons including, "Because my English was horrible to begin with. The linguistics. The way I would dress. They would even say the way I would smell. Somehow to them it was funny, I guess. I don't know where the funny part came from but to them it was. I never felt part of high school at all."

The only place Rafael felt safe was in the classroom of his English as a second language (ESL) teacher: "Her classroom was the safe haven for me. The only place where I could avoid bullying was in that classroom. Outside they were pushing me, they would do whatever they wanted with me. I always thank the teachers that opened their classrooms, especially during lunchtime." Rafael noted that, sadly, this kind of bullying still happens, which is a major reason he has stayed in his position at California State University, Fresno for 28 years, but it was not an obvious career choice for him at the beginning. Upon graduating from high school, Rafael recalls his dream was always to be like his dad: "He was a farmer and people looked up to him and people would seek him out for employment and for advice and for everything. I just thought, wow, I'm going to be like him. So, I wanted to be a farmer. That was my only goal. So, I never meant to go to college, never even crossed my mind."

Rafael ended up enrolling at California State University, Fresno but in an unexpected way. It began when he accompanied a friend who was interviewing at the university but was afraid to go alone. According to Rafael, "He needed somebody just to come with him. I said, 'Okay, I'll go to be your bodyguard.'" While waiting for his friend to come out of the interview, the program director came out of his office and asked Rafael if he was applying to college. When Rafael said no, he was just waiting for a friend, the program director insisted, "How come you're not applying?" to which Rafael replied, "I'm probably not going to get admitted." The program director told Rafael, "You know what, I'm the director. 'You apply and I will admit you,'" which led Rafael to complete his application on the spot.

Surprisingly, after an interview with the school counselor, Rafael was told that he was "not recommended" for admission. According to Rafael, "That tears me up. He didn't recommend me for admission to the university because of my language challenge. That was his excuse. He said 'linguistically, he is not ready.' I was mad. So, I waited, and I said, 'I've got to see the director.'" When the director came out of his office, Rafael said: "You know what, I don't like what you did to me. You made me do this application process just for you guys to tell me that I'm not admitted. I don't need this stuff." Surprised that Rafael was not recommended, the director took his paperwork, invited Rafael into his office, and said, "Look what I'm going to do." He then put "admitted" on Rafael's application, to which Rafael asked, "What does that mean?" The director replied: "You're ready to come to college."

It would have been easy for Rafael to leave the college angry and frustrated at his rejection, but through the care and belief of the director, Rafael's whole life changed, and he went on to change the lives of many others. After Rafael graduated from California State University, Fresno, he became an ESL teacher and tutor, helped found the College Assistant Migrant Program (CAMP) in 1987, and even started his own foundation for education and leadership, which provides education, civic engagement, and immigrant services. True to his values and his past, Rafael's foundation provides a free virtual university for immigrant, migrant, and undocumented parents.

ALBA, CAMILA, AND ELMIRA

Alba, Camila, and Elmira are sisters who all attended the teacher credential program at California State University, Fresno, and like Rafael were part of Mini Corps Program. Alba, Camila, and Elmira grew up in the Central Valley and attended the local elementary and high schools where they would eventually become teachers. As is typical of children from migrant families, Alba, Camila, and Elmira grew up in poverty, struggling with issues such as not being able to speak English, having low self-confidence, being told they were "dumb," falling prey to cultural stereotypes and prejudice about immigrants not being real Americans, and being subjected to the tyranny of low expectations both in school and in the workforce. Alba, Camila, and Elmira all benefited from having a CMC tutor, which eventually led them to want to be part of CMC themselves to help other migrant students, as they all aspired to be teachers. The sisters describe their journey to becoming teachers of color from poor, underserved, and minoritized backgrounds: "We're not the richest. But we are rich in values and love."

When asked what made them all want to become teachers, Camila jumped right in, "I think for me being able to relate to my students. I got to meet so many students who felt anxious and worried because they had that language barrier. And I was always there, and I'd be like: 'You're going to be okay. I know how you're feeling. I went through it too. I know you have Fs, but we're going to move them to Bs, and you can still be successful even though you're struggling right now.'" Alba agreed that having once been a student who struggled in school not only encouraged her to become a teacher but shaped the kind of teacher she became:

> For me, I have always wanted to be a teacher ever since I was little. I love the classroom environment. Just teaching something and then the students finally understanding it. I've been in the classroom sometimes, and students don't get what the teacher's doing. I'm like 'Okay, hold on. Let's look at it in a different way. What if we tried it this way?' And then they're like well, 'why didn't the teacher just say that?' I love those moments where you can kind of see it through different eyes. And we've all been students before one way or another, so we kind of put ourselves in those shoes.

Elmira, who also struggled in school herself, was initially more hesitant about becoming a teacher than her sisters were. She was eventually won over, however, when she found a role model and mentor who genuinely believed in her, and, like her sisters, realized the kind of impact she could have helping students like herself. As Elmira remembers: "Let me tell you I was not planning to be a teacher. I always said I was never going to be a teacher. In 3rd grade I still didn't know how to read. I struggled with reading. And sadly, I was one of those students who met a teacher who was very negative, and she told me that I was never going to learn, and I was very dumb. So, my self-esteem just went down the drain." As a result, Elmira would often stuff her homework deep inside of her backpack "where it became all wrinkled and not good anymore," and then tell her teachers that she left it at home. One day she had a teacher who took it out of her backpack and called her parents. According to Elmira, this experience was transformative. Yes, she got into trouble, but after that the teacher would work with her every day after school and even meet her at the school on Saturdays to help her succeed, encouraging her to stay in school and go on to college.

Elmira also shared a captivating story about a migrant family that experienced tragedy, which was fundamental in Elmira's decision to become a teacher. According to Elmira, "The whole family was in a car accident. The dad passed away and the mom lost one of her arms. The mom was still working in the fields. She would go and ask everyone for an opportunity. She was put down a lot of times by different managers who said, "No. No. How are you going to work? You only have one hand. You can't do this." Elmira met them after the accident and was tutoring both the son and daughter. According to Elmira, "They were having a very hard time. We would go and drop off food like fruit and vegetables and whatever we could get for them. The mom did not speak English. She did not know how to read or write. She pushed her children to get good grades. She would talk to the teachers and always have them translate or have the migrant teacher translate. She made sure they had straight A's."

Elmira continued to help the son even after he went to high school. One day he told her that he wanted to be a doctor, but that his mom had already told him that there was no money for him to go to college. He told Elmira, "We can't afford that. So, I'm actually starting a job as a janitor at the high school I go to next week. Look where we live. Look at everything the school does for us to help us. We don't have the financial stability to go to school. So, I'm going to start working in the fields with my mom." Elmira remembers thinking, "What do I do? What can I do to help this student?" Alongside her migrant teacher in the CMC program Elmira invited the mom to come have coffee at the school. According to Elmira, "I remember she brought little cookies, and she brought bread and we had coffee. We sat down, and the mom said: 'So, I heard my son wants to be a doctor. Yeah, my kids are so smart, and I know they would have done so many great things if we had the money to do so. But I already told them that high school is as high as they're going to go because it's free.' And we were like, 'Wait a minute. You need to hear all of this!'"

After they gave the mother information about financial aid and scholarships and told her about the migrant program at school her son could be part of, Elmira shares, "I'll never forget the lady crying and saying, 'I cannot believe I was going to keep my kids from going to school because I didn't know this. I cannot believe that these things happen because parents don't know.' She cried and thanked us so much." The son eventually got his bachelor's degree and recently bought a house for his mom and his sister and him. Elmira says that every time she sees her, the mom gets so emotional, telling Elmira, 'I will never know how to thank you for this. I'm so glad there's a program like yours because people would not know the things they know if you weren't there to inform them.'"

According to Elmira, "That's when I knew. I am so blessed to have teaching as my career because we can surely make a difference. I mean, we're not the richest, but we're rich in our values and love. We have lots of love." Her sister Alba similarly shared, "This program not only taught us to be professionals but also taught us to be humble and kind and remember our roots always so that we can help others who are like us and to not forget where we come from because we have the power to help so many people. And then we can help them so that they can help others too."

CORTEZ

When we met with Cortez, he was in his final year of student teaching in the teacher education program at California State University, Fresno. Like many of the candidates we interviewed, he was born in Mexico and came to the United States when he was 10 years old and in the 5th grade, settling in the community of Mendota, about 45 minutes aways from Fresno, where the population is 100% agricultural and Latinx. Even though it took Cortez 3 years to learn the language and get fully integrated into the classroom, he spoke highly of his teachers, who were the only "professionals" (people who did not work in the fields) he was exposed to. According to Cortez, "I saw in my teachers a lot of concern for the students. They developed clubs. I was in the mountain biking club. I was in the history club. And I was part of those clubs without even knowing the language. My teachers were really concerned with getting me there, with integrating me into the classroom."

Cortez credits his 8th-grade history teacher as changing his educational trajectory, noting that "We have become lifelong friends because he was the one who pushed me from English learner classes to the mainstream classroom. He said you can do it. He pushed me to it. He went and talked to the principal and said, 'You know what? Cortez is ready for the mainstream classroom. He's got to do it.'" As a result of this positive experience in school, Cortez always saw teaching as being his career choice. He came straight from high school to California State University, Fresno. Cortez recalls that decision, "You know what? For me just coming to college was a big accomplishment. I'm one out of eight children that ever finished high school, and then just being accepted into university was really big for me and my family."

Cortez applied to both Oregon State and California State University, Fresno. While he got accepted to both, he decided to stay home to be close to his parents, a decision common among many low-income and immigrant candidates with whom we spoke. According to Cortez, he needed to stay close to his parents because, "I'm usually the one that drives them around. I'm the one that takes care of them." When asked what he thought the hardest part of becoming a teacher was, Cortez responded, "I think just the time and effort it takes and then just getting there. It's really hard because of finances. That's been my biggest challenge. Every summer I go to Alaska to work in the fishing industry, and I get some money over there and I budget throughout the year. But without that it would be almost impossible just to be in the credential program and without financial aid, of course."

When asked about some of the other challenges Cortez experienced in the teacher education program, he described how difficult it was coming from a rural area. Cortez spoke of the attitude of the teachers he trained under, many of whom believed that low-income, rural, and migrant parents do not care much about their children's education. According to Cortez, the issue is much more complicated. He reflects on the rural parents he worked with: "Their attitude is they want their kids to get an education, but they don't know the details. I mean they don't know math because some of them didn't even go to school and have never been to a school. They don't know English and they don't know any subjects. So, when they go to school and the teacher asks, 'Do you have any questions about your child's education,' they're not going to have any questions because they don't know."

Cortez has decided that when he graduates from California State University, Fresno, he is going to teach in a rural area like where he grew up. He hopes to become the kind of teacher who will reach out to rural parents, welcoming them into the school and influencing other teachers to do the same. This is something Cortez feels is his "responsibility as a teacher." When we asked Cortez how he would convince a group of young Latino men in high school that teaching would be a good option for them, he vividly recalled some of the migrant students he had helped stay in school and progress academically: "I would tell a group of Latino students being a teacher gives you the chance to change your community and that's empowering." Cortez underscored that many migrant students believe that they must make a choice between college or "the fields" and that there is "nothing in between." Cortez shared that "I want them to know there's something in-between. I think every career counts and I think every job out there should be validated. So, it's just the exposure to them and just making them think about what they want to do gives them a better spectrum of where they want to be."

Having founded an after-school cosmetology club in his old high school, Cortez notes that in addition to providing vocational guidance, part of the club's purpose is to explore issues of self-esteem: "In that club we do talk about topics of how beauty is perceived in various parts of the world. We do have that academic discussion of what it means to be beautiful or whatnot." In conclusion, Cortez emphasized how important it was to meet the needs of his students: "Curriculum comes and goes, and it's the same thing recycled over and over again. I think just meeting the needs of your students is more important. Having a goal at the end and having those students meet that goal and doing something with their lives. I saw a lot of my friends just in the fields and they're still working out there in the fields. It is a little concerning because I know they had the potential to go to school, to get an education. Again, it's just that exposure."

DEAN

Dean was a sophomore at Jackson State University when we first met him. Although he was born in Indiana, Dean told us that "During my high school career, I had made different goals that I wanted to accomplish. One was I wanted to attend an HBCU. I wanted to experience the South and I wanted to get away from home." While Dean got accepted to several schools, he did not have the money to pay for his tuition. According to Dean, "At that time, I didn't think of Jackson State as an option." His mother suggested he look deeper into Jackson State because his oldest brother had gone there for a year before he joined the military. Dean was able to send in the paperwork, call people, and received late admission. He credits his mom's help with his being able to receive a scholarship, making Jackson State affordable.

At first Dean was not interested in a career in teaching, but after attending an information session about Call Me MISTER, he reconsidered. Call Me MISTER (which is discussed more thoroughly in other chapters of this book) is a cohort program that originated at Clemson University, a PWI in South Carolina, and was designed to attract Black men into the teaching profession. The program pays for their college tuition and many other expenses, while providing candidates with extra mentoring and support. In exchange, candidates do community service and agree to stay and teach in local schools for several years upon graduation. The program has received a significant amount of attention due to its success in increasing the small number of Black men who pursue teaching. Dean, however, recalls being skeptical when he first heard about it: "It so happened that during the undecided major orientation, our supervisor was talking about the Call Me MISTER program. I talked with him for a while and asked him question after question, like really drilling the program to make sure it was ethical. Everything checked out so I went through the process, interviewed and I'm in the Call Me MISTER program. Thus began my major interest in teaching."

When asked why he thought Call Me MISTER might not be ethical, Dean explained, "At first it sounded like it was too good to be true. The way he was talking about it he was saying that the benefits that came with the program were that your tuition and books are going to be paid for." Once convinced that the program was legitimate, Dean enrolled. When asked if he ever had African American men as teachers in his own education, Dean replied, "African American teachers? None that I can recall. In elementary school we had a vice principal who was an African American man. Sometimes I would see him in the classroom in place of a teacher but in that actual position, no." When asked if he thought it was important for an African American man such as himself to be in front of the classroom, Dean shared, "Yes, I think it's important if I can do my job well. I think that having an African American man in the classroom, I'm going to call it a rare sight." According to Dean, "The main reason the teacher is there is to help give students knowledge so they can learn and be able to do more with the knowledge that they're given. It just takes time." So, when asked why he cared about teaching, Dean proudly answered, "Why do I care? As I thought about that question, what was just flashing through my mind were different people that I've run into, different children, even adults, who I have been able to teach something new. As I thought about that I realized that teaching is important to me because it's always happening. I don't think you can get away from it whether you're teaching yourself or teaching other people."

KIM

Kim was an education major at Stone Child College who was born locally and raised by her grandparents. Her late grandfather worked in a school for over 30 years. He was both a bus driver and a paraprofessional. According to Kim, "He was a jack of all trades at the school." Her great-grandfather was one of the first employees at Rocky Boy school on the reservation. Many other members of Kim's family were also educators, including her aunts and uncles and her grandmother. According to Kim, "Just seeing how my grandparents, my uncles and my aunties and seeing how the students took to them in school. It was something. So, my biggest goal has always been to teach at Rocky Boy and just kind of keep the family thing going."

After having children at an early age, Kim decided to enroll in Stone Child College, a Tribal College that served her reservation, sharing that "It's just convenient because we have the childcare center here, plus I just like the atmosphere here." When asked what specifically she liked about her experience at Stone Child College, Kim responded that the small classes and collaborative atmosphere were a big draw for her: "It isn't hard for us to go ask a question and get an answer. Our class is so small, and we could help each other."

When asked why she wanted to be a teacher, Kim shared more about her desire to be a role model for other Native American children, including the positive response she had already received as a student teacher from the Native community: "We have parent teacher conferences and parents coming in and out of the school picking up their kids. There's always compliments coming from people like 'I'm so glad you're doing this.' 'I'm so glad you're in the school.' 'It's nice to see a Native face in the school.' 'It's nice to have a positive Native role model for my kids to look up to.' There's been a lot of that. So that really gives you that feeling that you're doing something right and that you can make a difference with the kids."

Kim further reflected on this connection: "What I've noticed about being a Native teacher in a Native school is that the kids can really relate to me. I find that some of the students who have been in that class all year come up to me some days and they're hugging me and hanging on my arms and hanging around my desk. They really open up and tell you things. There's been a lot of things that make you sad to hear, including personal experiences from the kids. I share a lot of that with my cooperating teacher. There's a lot that they have opened up to me about that she hasn't heard. I think that's kind of just the level of comfortability of the kids seeing one of us and not just another White teacher." According to Kim, "That's been one of the biggest things for me is just the community wide support I feel. It is a big deal to receive a college education on the reservation here. There's not that many people with bachelors' degrees or even associate degrees. To be able to put that to use and to feel that you're making a difference and to have people supporting you in what you're doing is always reassuring."

Kim felt that the support she received from the surrounding community gave her an extra push to finish her degree, reflecting that many students on the reservation see graduating high school as their top goal. According to Kim, "So you see a lot of students graduate high school and then that's it. They don't pursue any other kind of education. When we finish, I'll be the first person from my graduating class at Box Elder High School to receive a bachelor's degree." Kim seemed conflicted about this: "I'm pretty proud of the fact, but then again at the same time it's sad to think there were 20 of us that graduated and there's maybe two or three students that have associates degrees. That's as far as they've gone."

Part of her motivation in becoming a teacher is to inspire more students from the reservation to go to college. "It's nice to think we can change that. I'm sure it's on all our minds to instill in these children at a young age to set the bar higher, to not look at high school graduation as a major life goal. It's one that can be built upon and that hopefully others can continue and try to do something with their lives." While Kim was not suggesting that children on the reservation were not ambitious, most ended up in construction jobs that were not fulfilling or sustainable. According to Kim, "It's kind of hard to explain but it is kind of different growing up on the reservation and seeing all the kids talking about what they want to be when they grow up. I've seen what happened to my generation and I just want to help the next line of kids that are coming up. I want to help them try to become something, I guess, and try to teach them to reach their goals and to set the bar high."

Kim concluded our talk by lamenting that many Native American students as young as kindergarten still identify themselves as White, suggesting that assimilation is still present in the school system. She noted that it was especially important for the students to have role models from their own culture: "I think it goes to show that it all goes hand in hand. They can relate to me. I'm not the darkest person. I'm not the most Native looking person, but there's something that they are relating to." Kim recalled telling a group of 6th-grade students they could do anything they wanted. She knew that most would end up working on the roads, but she wanted to impress upon them that there were other options. One young man student said that he wanted to be a doctor or something like that but didn't think he'd be able to do it. When she asked him why, he changed his mind and said he believed he could do it after all because, "You're from here and you went and did it." As Kim remembers, "So he starts writing all these things in his journal and pretty soon everybody started writing in their journals. I almost started crying. I thought, I only have a little bit of time left with these guys."

SETH

Seth is a liberal arts faculty member at Stone Child College who shared his unusual trajectory with us. A White man, he worked at the Rocky Boy schools while getting his bachelor's degree in education in the 1970s. Stone Child College approached him in 1994, hiring him to be a program coordinator. After a stint in the school district as a principal, Seth returned to Stone Child College as an assistant dean just as the current president passed away. As Seth recalls, "I remember walking into the board meeting because at that time, I was the dean of academics, and I was to present the faculty evaluations and my recommendations. As I walked in, they said, 'Congratulations to you' I said, 'For what?' They said: 'You're now the president.' They had had the discussion prior to me walking in and said that they decided to offer that in the interim until they could find somebody to replace the previous president."

Seth thought about it: "It was extremely trying conditions at that time. Do I really want to do this to myself? I knew the amount of work that was going to have to be done." Reluctantly, Seth agreed and began to map out exactly what had to be done, which he found to be "kind of a daunting task." According to Seth, "We had fiscal issues. We had accreditation that was coming up. We had just a series of problems. We had facilities that were woefully inept as far as educational facilities. That had to be addressed. There was a lot of work that had to be done. 'They said, okay, you're the man now.' There wasn't a day that went by in the first six months that I didn't think 'what the heck did you do to yourself?' Every day it was crisis management. You had to look at it that way because of the enormity of the problems that we had to face."

As he explained, Seth was able to make some significant changes, including securing more funding for the college: "There were a couple of very good agreements that we struck between the land grant institutions recognizing the Tribal Colleges as a land grant institution and the executive order recognizing the Tribal Colleges. Both of those in themselves were immensely powerful for us. That gave us the power to walk back to these departments, walk back to our representatives and say 'Here, you've got to step to the plate here. You can't ignore this when it's been signed by the president as far as our executive order and land grant status. You can't ignore this.' It did really open up a lot of doors for funding that we otherwise wouldn't have had the opportunity to."

While Seth was transparent about the challenges many of the students at Stone Child College face—such as poverty, alcoholism, prescription drug abuse and low self-worth—he also was cognizant of the discrimination against Native Americans and stereotyping that still occurs in the broader community. When we asked why he thought many Native Americans had a low sense of self-worth, he responded, "It's engrained. Anywhere they go publicly they are what they are. They're not extremely well received in other communities. In shopping communities, Great Falls, for example, it's not really a border community but it's close enough because that's the nearest great shopping area. They have highly misguided ideas of Native Americans in our outlying communities."

While Seth was not Native American, he did grow up in the local community and went to the local high school as one of five other White students. In high school, Seth remembers playing football on "the only Indian team in the area" and having had community members say "derogatory comments" in the gym, such as, "You dirty stinking Indian, go back to the res where you belong." While Seth believes these kinds of messages are "more subliminal now," he feels strongly that "it's not as open but it's still there." Recalling a time recently that he and some students were in Great Falls and stopped to eat lunch, Seth shares, "Our waitress said two derogatory things about Native Americans within, what, seven or eight minutes." Seth added, "She was laughing the whole time she was saying it as if it didn't even matter." According to Seth, "You keep trying to tell them they are some of the best people I've ever been around in my entire life from right here, great people, wonderful people. But you never see them because you don't want to see them. What you want to see is that drunk Indian walking down the street and you don't spend the time to try to find out there are some great people. So, it's an uphill battle. You're talking about self-worth, that's what these kids grew up with. You just get angry with the situation because they could be anything they wanted to be."

Although it was only meant to be an interim appointment, Seth stayed in the presidency until 2004, eventually returning to the college, teaching remedial math, speech, English, and history. He is involved in the teacher education program at Stone Child College and was one of the faculty members advocating that the program expand from a 2-year program to a 4-year program—the first in the college's history. Seth emphasized how important it is to create a 4-year program so that candidates do not have to leave their homes and communities to finish their bachelor's degree. According to Seth, "At one point there was less than 2% of the students who left the reservation to earn their baccalaureate degree who succeeded." Stone Child College is bringing teacher education home.

These are just some of the stories of the faculty members and candidates we spoke with. While each story is unique, it is hard not to notice the common thread upon which going to college and having a professional career was considered out of reach for so many aspiring teachers of color. They grappled with finding jobs that would allow them to immediately support their families over jobs that required a higher degree, and they faced multiple obstacles, including bullying and racial prejudice. Merely getting into college was a huge accomplishment for many of the teacher educators and candidates we talked to, but as these stories attest, their persistence and resilience paid off. It is important to underscore that many times they succeeded due to one person who believed in them, supported them, protected them, and/or inspired them. Most importantly, these stories illuminate the importance of diversifying the curriculum, allowing teachers and students of all backgrounds to feel validated and to take pride in their cultural heritage. In the next chapter, we explore how MSIs have integrated culturally relevant pedagogy across their entire teacher education programs.

CHAPTER 3

Changing the Narrative
What Does Culturally Relevant Pedagogy Look Like in Action?

> Unfortunately, the tacos and sombreros and Native American teepees appear to be at the forefront of what teachers will do, which does not really deal with the whole idea of multicultural education. What we need to try and inculcate into our teachers is an understanding of institutional racism, [and] systemic types of inequities that occur in the educational process. You may find some superficial changes in terms of science books where you see more Black kids or Native American kids in the chapters, but there is not a real effort to change the narrative.
>
> —Prentice Baptiste, professor of education, New Mexico State University

In this chapter, we focus on the ways that students of color are often seen through a deficit lens, and how the ways that we prepare candidates to teach them can likewise rely on stereotypes, biases, and assumptions that devalue the nuanced and meaningful cultural capital, knowledge, and aspirations that students of color bring with them into the classroom. More specifically, we address the following questions: What is culturally relevant pedagogy? What does it mean to prepare candidates for "asset-based" teaching and learning? How does self-reflection help guide this process? How do MSIs tailor the teacher education curriculum to the unique demographics of the communities they serve and reside in? How do MSIs use intersectionality as a way of acknowledging systemic racism while still challenging stereotypes and assumptions specific to different identity groups? How do MSIs integrate these principles and practices across their entire teacher education programs, including coursework and clinical practice? We also provide specific examples from our research of culturally relevant pedagogy (CRP) at MSIs, taking into consideration that even within the MSI designation these institutions vary in terms of their founding missions, as well as the primary student demographics and communities they serve. While CRP is grounded in certain characteristics and commitments that transcend individual educational contexts, as this chapter demonstrates, it can still look different in practice at an HBCU, an HSI, an AANAPISI, or a TCU.

Moreover, it is critical that both teacher educators and candidates learn to see students in intersectional ways. When considering how to design and use CRP, candidates must recognize the ways in which students have more than one static cultural identity and thus cannot be easily compartmentalized or given a standardized curriculum based only on their assumed race. For example, many of the students in the schools where teacher candidates in this study worked were multilingual and/or multiracial, came from low-income families in heavily rural or urban communities, were children of immigrants or migrants, or grew up on a reservation. Culturally relevant, also called culturally proficient, teachers understand the importance of getting to really know their students, including their current families, generational ancestors, and communities, to craft a curriculum that is engaging, relevant, and historically accurate.

Equally important, teacher educators and candidates need to understand that acknowledging diversity is not the same thing as challenging racist practices and systemic inequities. CRP requires teachers do much more than simply add a few texts by people of color to the curriculum, include a "heroes and holidays" unit, and/or give students a chance to share something from their culture. While these strategies are significant, they do not go far enough. Students need to understand why they were left out of the curriculum to begin with, as well as how to challenge narratives in textbooks and other materials that are inaccurate or incomplete regarding the experiences of racialized minorities in the United States and around the globe.

We seek to challenge the current model of teacher education—discussed in Chapter 1—where racial and cultural diversity is seen as an add-on or subfield of teaching. Each of the four examples we provide approaches CRP from a different perspective. When we examine CRP at Stone Child College, we illustrate the ways in which the entire teacher education program is organized by and modeled after the Chippewa Cree culture. More specifically, the four phases of the teacher education program align with the four seasons depicted on the Cree Medicine Wheel. In our discussion of CRP at California State University, Fresno, on the other hand, we explore a specific assignment in the candidate's Culturally and Linguistically Sustaining Pedagogy course, where candidates reflect on their own cultural heritages using art, video, and personal narratives to create artifacts of what teaching in California's Central Valley, their home, means to them. By contrast, when we examine CRP at Jackson State University, we do not focus on program organization or course content, but on how candidates learn to relate to their students in culturally relevant ways. In this case, CRP is embodied in how Black teachers learn to serve as role models and mentors for Black students, approaching them from an asset-based perspective that acknowledges their cultural wealth and capital. Finally, at New Mexico State University we profile a research assignment in the candidates' multicultural education course in which they are asked to choose a school and spend 12 weeks in the surrounding community, talking to diverse community members, physically mapping the community structures and resources, and researching census data and other relevant statistics about the community. This assignment serves to help teacher education candidates to personally experience and analyze systemic inequities, which have an impact on the everyday lives of students, while simultaneously learning to bridge students' and community knowledge with the school curriculum.

In addition, while this chapter provides concrete examples of what CRP looks like in practice at each of the four institutions we researched, we will continue to discuss CRP in the other chapters of this book given that it is inherently connected to building peer support and using cohort models in teacher education (Chapter 4); creating opportunities for candidates to bridge coursework with practice through spending quality time working in authentic and diverse school settings (Chapter 5); and having candidates engage with parents and surrounding communities through servant leadership, community service, and practitioner inquiry (Chapter 6).

WHAT IS CULTURALLY RELEVANT PEDAGOGY?

The concept of CRP can be traced to educator Gloria Ladson-Billings, who coined the term in her 1995 article "Towards a Theory of Culturally Relevant Pedagogy," published in the *American Educational Research Journal*. Challenging deficit-based assumptions as to why African American students did not do as well in school as their White peers, Ladson-Billings underscored that effective pedagogical practice needs to help students "accept and affirm their cultural identity while developing critical perspectives that challenge inequities that schools (and other institutions) perpetuate" (p. 469).

As Ladson-Billings built out the meaning of the term, she further noted that CRP must provide a way for students "to maintain their cultural integrity while succeeding academically" (p. 475), and that culturally relevant teachers are educators that must believe all students are capable of academic success. To facilitate CRP, teachers need to strategically build bridges between students' cultures and content knowledge, and assessment must be multifaceted, incorporating multiple forms of excellence (p. 481). Anticipating the question, "Isn't what you described just good teaching?" Ladson-Billings responded that maybe so, but: "Why does so little of it seem to occur in classrooms populated by African American students?" (p. 484).

While Ladson-Billings focused on African American students, the concept of CRP has since grown to include students of all cultural backgrounds and identities. In the years since Ladson-Billings' article was published, the term CRP has not only persisted; there have been several variations on it including, most prominently, culturally responsive pedagogy, culturally revitalizing pedagogy, and culturally sustaining pedagogy. While the differences between these terms are not huge, they are significant. Paris (2012), for example, suggests that the concepts of culturally relevant or responsive pedagogy do not go "far enough" (p. 95). His suggested use of the term "culturally sustaining pedagogy" has a greater focus on activism, social transformation, and systemic change, tying teaching to democratic ideals (Paris, 2012). According to Paris (2012), culturally sustaining pedagogy emphasizes the explicit goal of perpetuating, fostering, and of course sustaining "linguistic, literate, and cultural pluralism as part of the democratic project of schooling" (p. 95). Paris further suggests:

> We must ask ourselves if the research and practice being produced under the umbrella of cultural relevance and responsiveness is, indeed, ensuring maintenance of the languages and cultures of African American, Latina/o, Indigenous American, Asian American, Pacific Islander American, and other longstanding, and newcomer communities in our classrooms. Furthermore, we must ask if a critical stance toward and critical action against unequal power relations is resulting from such research and practice. (2012, pp. 94–95)

Paris expresses his concern that the term "relevant" might encourage teachers to add a text or two that reflects the history and experience of a racial or cultural group without ever challenging why those texts were not included in the first place. In other words, a teacher could be culturally relevant without ever bringing up key issues of colonialism, genocide, segregation, and forced assimilation. Two years later (2014), Ladson-Billings agreed with Paris, noting that:

> My work on culturally relevant pedagogy has taken on a life of its own, and what I see in the literature and sometimes in practice is totally unrecognizable to me. What state departments, school districts and individual teachers are now calling "culturally relevant pedagogy" is often a distortion and corruption of the central ideas I attempted to promulgate. . . . to name and define culturally sustaining pedagogy will need to be a vigilant and steadfast project that guards against the degradation of the meaning and implementation of the term. (p. 82)

Ladson Billings was right to be concerned, as the term "culturally relevant pedagogy" has become somewhat of a buzzword across education and is often used to describe any form of teaching that even mentions race or cultural diversity. The bottom line is that whether you call it culturally relevant, responsive, or sustaining, this pedagogy is a cohesive theory of teaching and learning that includes several fundamental and intersectional components including using students' existing strengths to drive instruction, assessment, and curriculum design (Gay, 2010); bridging students' home knowledge with in-school learning (Moll et al., 1992); rejecting deficit perspectives on students and communities of color (Gay, 2010; Yosso, 2005); establishing an ethic of care in the classroom that extends to students' families and home communities (Noddings, 1992); engaging students in critical reflection about their own lives and the societies they live in (Aronson & Laughter, 2016); actively challenging and disrupting institutional racism in schools (Paris, 2012; Valenzuela, 2016); and refusing to accept anything but students' highest potential (Howard, 2001). In summary, CRP is less about a particular lesson plan or text and more about the way teachers regard, treat, and engage diverse students.

CULTURALLY RELEVANT PEDAGOGY AND MSIs

The practice of CRP has long been a hallmark of MSIs, even if they have not all adopted that term (Conrad & Gasman, 2017; Petchauer & Mawhinney, 2017; Gasman et al., 2017). As discussed in the introduction, MSIs were founded with and/or share in the mission of providing a robust educational experience to students of color that sets them up for academic success while validating their cultures and empowering their communities (Conrad & Gasman, 2017). They are further distinguished by the fact that they hire large numbers of faculty of color, attract students from local neighborhoods and communities, and prioritize teaching and student relationships over research.

As noted in the introduction, MSIs have a long history of innovative teacher education. In 2000, the Alliance for Equity in Education promoted the unique role of MSIs in preparing the next generation of teachers in their report "Educating the Emerging Majority: The Role of Minority-Serving Institutions in Confronting America's Teacher Crisis." According to the authors:

> Whether the focus is on African Americans, Hispanics, or American Indians, the missions of all MSIs embrace the needs of the communities they serve. The commitment to supporting cultural values and traditions and to preserving and recognizing the past even as they strive to make an impact on the future sets MSIs apart from mainstream institutions. (2000, p. 16)

Recent research has confirmed that MSIs are still in the forefront of creating new models for teacher education that reject the more superficial melting-pot approach to diversity that persists at many PWIs. For example, as Petchauer and Mawhinney note in *Teacher Education Across Minority-Serving Institutions* (2017):

> MSIs build their missions and educational approach around the social and economic barriers low-income students and students of color often experience. . . . MSIs also create comprehensive and nurturing environments that advocate for academic development connected to racial self-development. (p. 3)

MSIs' authentic commitment to preparing teachers in culturally relevant ways led Petchauer and Mawhinney (2017) to conclude that "MSIs have done much more than help increase racial diversity in the teacher's lounge," calling attention to MSIs' contributions to innovations in teacher education program design and effectiveness (p. 5).

In a recent report, *Preparing Teachers for Diverse Schools*, Marchitello & Trinidad (2019) agree that MSIs "intentionally design their education programs to serve communities of color" and urge that "other schools of education and teacher preparation programs can learn from MSIs' extensive experience and expertise in successfully preparing teacher candidates to work effectively in diverse schools" (p. 11). The authors further note that "The equity and social justice missions of MSIs attract both students and faculty with a similarly strong commitment to those goals. As such, discussing the role and consequences of racism, sexism, and other forms of discrimination is commonplace and often a central part of education at MSIs" (p. 15).

It is important to point out, however, that even within the designation of MSI, there are many different strategies that reflect different institutional histories, cultures, and demographics. Teacher education at HBCUs, for example, reflects HBCUs' unique history as institutions founded to support Black education and Black teacher education during segregation. Dilworth (2012) has called attention to the fact that "Although HBCUs are a subset of all postsecondary institutions, their historical roots bind them in significant ways" (p. 121). Similarly, culturally relevant pedagogy at TCUs, which were founded with a mission to serve Native American students, pay close attention to the impact of forced colonization and the need for a curriculum that is aligned with Native American cultural and spiritual values. By contrast, most HSIs and AANAPISIs were previously PWIs that earned their MSI designation because of the changing demographics of the student body. At these institutions, culturally relevant pedagogy often focuses on issues of immigration and English language only policies.

In the remainder of this chapter, we explore some of the specific ways in which culturally relevant pedagogy is integrated into the teacher education programs of the institutions we studied.

A PLACE OF HOPE AND HEALING: CULTURALLY RELEVANT PEDAGOGY AT STONE CHILD COLLEGE

Indigenous Peoples around the world have challenged colonization and the imposition of whiteness as property; we have resisted, not accepted, the normativity of whiteness. Resistance, however, is taxing on mind, body, and spirit. As we tell our stories and speak our words, we heal ourselves and reclaim our humanity and knowledge about the world around us. (Haynes-Writer, 2008, p. 10)

What makes us unique is that we provide a culturally relevant education that embodies our tribal cultural values, our history, our language and of course the contemporary issues that we face.... It's important to look at our potential in terms of our growth and what we see as future opportunities.... It's a prominent place, and the aesthetic here is important not only to our culture but how we see what I often call the place of hope.

—Nathaniel St. Pierre, former president, Stone Child College

On the Rocky Boy Indian Reservation in Montana, about 40 miles from the U.S.–Canada border, residents come from the Chippewa Cree Tribe, which was established in 1916. Almost 70 years later, in 1984, Stone Child College (SSC) became a federally designated Tribal College dedicated to serving students from the Chippawa Cree Tribe. Accordingly, SCC's teacher education program is designed around honoring and preserving Chippewa Cree language, history, and values. Considering a long history of colonization and forced assimilation, having dedicated schools on their reservation with teachers who come from the local community, along with a teacher education program that is fully aligned with Chippewa Cree tribal culture, is no small feat. TCUs like SCC have been at the center of re-envisioning teacher education programs. Lansing (2014) describes them as "places where the next generation of teachers may be invited to 'remain Indian' and are empowered to generate a culturally responsive education for the children and families they serve" (pp. 39–40).

When we visited SCC to collect data for our research on teacher education at MSIs, the teacher education program was expanding from a 2-year program to a 4-year program. Once completed, it became the first 4-year program in SCC's history. Previously, teacher candidates would have to transfer to a 4-year school to complete their coursework, do their student teaching, and receive their certification. Most candidates went to Montana State University–Northern (Northern), a large predominantly White state college about 30 miles north of the Rocky Boy Reservation. Others took advantage of an articulation agreement between Stone Child College and another Tribal College, Salish Kooteni College, which was over 350 miles away, to finish their teaching degrees. Either way, it was very disruptive for aspiring teachers to have to transfer to another school midway through their training, and many complained that the preparation they were receiving was not aligned with their tribal culture and values. As one candidate reflected on leaving SCC to complete his degree at Northern: "For me being in a class at Northern with 80 other students in there, I was kind of shy. I was just another kid in the back. If there was something I didn't fully understand it was hard for me to just reach out to the teacher or to the instructor, professor and I would kind of just get lost. It's almost like a ripple effect. When you get lost on one thing, you're just further and further behind."

By contrast, being able to complete one's entire teacher preparation at SCC not only enabled candidates to do their clinical practice in local schools on the Rocky Boy Reservation where most candidates grew up and still live, it has demonstrated a clear investment in the education and preservation of Chippewa Cree culture. According to a faculty member and teacher education program director at SCC, who was one of the architects of expanding the 4-year program:

> The candidates really do become culturally relevant teachers. You can't teach them that in the first two years and then send them off to a state college that wants nothing. I mean the state college gives it lip service, but they aren't doing it. And so, in our program, every single lesson plan, if they go out and teach it, it has to have culture in it.

Teacher candidates we interviewed at SCC were likewise acutely aware of the impact they have as Native teachers, who are authentically using CRP in reservation schools. As one candidate in the program shared with us, "I noticed, being a Native teacher in a Native school, kids can really relate to me." Having Native teachers represented in reservation schools is deeply significant, as many PWI teacher education programs continue to rely on myths and stereotypes about Native cultures, deficit-based assumptions about Native students' academic ability and resilience, and ignorance about many of the fundamental values and concepts that comprise Native American identity, ways of knowing, interacting, and learning. By contrast, TCUs offer candidates opportunities for authentic practice in Native schools along with meaningful engagement with tribal families and communities. Not only does the new 4-year program at SCC, for example, allow for candidates to stay in close physical proximity to the Rocky Boy tribal community and schools, but also professors and support staff in the program go to great lengths to create and model curriculum and pedagogy that is in harmony with Native culture, values, and spirituality, such as through working collaboratively, emphasizing experiential learning, honoring oral histories, engaging families, and learning from tribal elders.

The curriculum for SCC's teacher education program is, in fact, intricately designed around the Cree Medicine Wheel, which depicts the four

Figure 3.1. Cree Medicine Wheel As Aligned With SCC Teacher Education Program

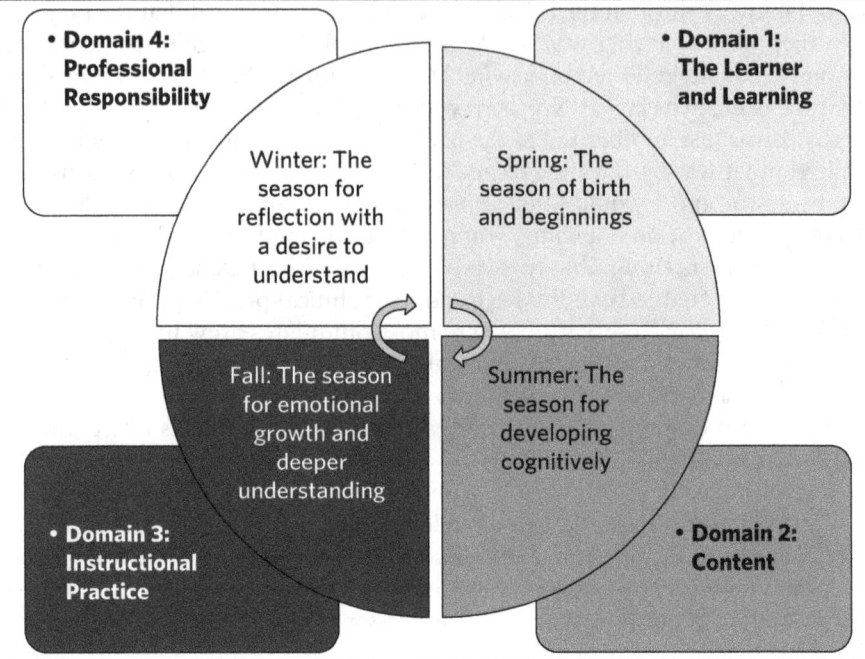

domains and seasons of Chippewa Cree culture (see Figure 3.1). Each domain is relevant and applicable to one module of SCC's teacher education program.

Domain 1, for example, is aligned to the spring season, which in Cree culture represents birth and beginnings. Thus, in Domain 1, SCC's teacher education program focuses on the learner. Among the expectations for candidates in Domain 1 are that the candidates value diverse languages and cultures and seek to integrate them into their instructional practice to engage students in learning, and the candidates make learners feel valued and help them learn to value each other. In Cree culture, the summer season is the time for cognitive growth and developing mental capabilities. Domain 2 thus ensures that teacher candidates have the content knowledge needed to effectively teach, including that the candidates value flexible learning environments that encourage learner exploration, discovery, and expression across content areas, and the candidates keep abreast of new ideas and understandings in the field.

Domain 3, which represents the fall season in Cree culture, is a time for emotional growth and deeper understanding. During Domain 3, candidates focus on instructional practice, including that the candidates value the variety of ways people communicate and encourage learners to develop and use multiple forms of communication, and the candidates value flexibility and reciprocity in the teaching process as necessary for adapting instruction to learner responses, ideas, and needs. Finally, Domain 4 represents the winter season, which is a time for reflection with a desire to understand. During this period, teacher candidates focus on enhancing their professional development and leadership skills: the candidates take responsibility for contributing to and advancing the profession, and the candidates see themselves as a learner, continuously seeking opportunities to use action research data and results as sources of analysis and reflection to improve practice.

Like the other MSIs we visited, the teacher preparation curriculum at SCC also engages candidates in critical exploration of their own educational roots and allows for them to spend quality time in authentic classrooms observing teachers and students. In the Introduction to Education course, for example, faculty take candidates back to the local schools where most of them went as children and have them reflect on the following questions: What is the teacher doing? What did they do to keep the attention of students? How did they correct a student who had gotten off track? What did you see in the classroom that maybe you didn't like? According to one faculty member, "In all of our courses, we try to get them into an actual classroom." She further shares that this is particularly important for aspiring Native American teachers because:

> I think their culture is naturally quiet. Their culture is to wait and see. And that's the opposite of White culture. We jump right in and then try to dig our way out. They're not going to just jump into stuff. It takes a little bit more. I think some of them are very insecure, and they don't really want to go into the classroom and work with the kids until they are done with their degree. I said it doesn't work like that. You don't automatically become a professional because you've got a piece of paper. You become a professional as you practice, practice, practice.

The shyness and hesitancy this faculty member describes when talking about the Native American candidates in SCC's program is partially reflective of their culture, and partially a result of the way that their culture has been colonized and marginalized throughout U.S. history, creating historical intergenerational trauma. Many candidates shared stories of their parents and grandparents who were forced to attend boarding schools in the late 19th and early 20th centuries—those set up by the federal government and Christian missionaries where they were separated from the parents, forced to abandon their tribal cultures and values, and only allowed to speak English.

While the official boarding school policies are over, research suggests that Native education at off-reservation public schools has not changed significantly as public education offered to Native American children still promotes a culture of assimilation using curriculum and pedagogy that is grounded in White history and values. This model is both ineffective and alienating for Indigenous students (McCarty & Lee, 2014; Lee, 2011). Native students still perform two to three grade levels below their White peers in reading and mathematics. The most recent estimates from the National Center for Education Statistics indicate that about 1 in 10 Native American students do not receive their high school diploma (De Brey et al., 2021). Similarly, their persistence through degree attainment in postsecondary settings is lower than all other ethnic groups in the United States (Lopez, 2017). Acutely aware of these statistics, professors and program staff at SCC shared with us their belief that teaching in Native communities is intimately bound up in "survival," "healing," and "hope." As one professor in SCC's program described it:

> Native culture is a survival culture. For Natives there [is] no separation between that spirit and that life. I have to teach too, but a lot of what I do is do healing. I think classrooms are great places to heal. Their spirits are gone, they've lost that because of the genocide. So, it's up to them to bring it back and then they can decide whether they really want to be Native or White. The ones that make it learn I could be Native in my own home, Native in my heart, Native in my spirit. . . . Native is a personal way of being. It's not white. It's a way. It's a spirit. It's a way of being.

The belief that being Native is something in one's heart and spirit summed up much of our research at SCC. According to one candidate in SCC's program: "I always think some of these kids if they understand who they are and where they come from, I feel like that will spark a better interest in their education and they will want to move forward." Another candidate added that their students are comfortable "seeing us as one of them and not just as another White teacher." In addition, candidates in SCC's teacher education program spoke often of how receptive local schools, students, and their families were to having Native American teachers on-site, such as the candidate who shared:

> We have parent teacher conferences and parents coming in and out of the school picking up their kids. There's always compliments coming from people like: "I'm so glad you're doing this. I'm so glad you're in the school. It's nice to see a Native face in the school. It's nice to have a positive Native role model for my kids to look up to." So that really gives you that feeling that you're doing something right and that you can make a difference with the kids. That's been one of the biggest things for me is just the community wide support I feel.

In sum, SCC's emphasis on preparing candidates to be culturally relevant and responsive teachers for Indigenous students offers hope that a new generation of teachers can reverse many of the negative academic statistics that currently characterize Native schools and students, such as high dropout rates and low standardized test scores (Brayboy & Castagno, 2009). SCC takes a holistic approach to this goal by creating culturally inviting community spaces where all candidates feel welcome, such as weekly drum ceremonies; honoring and preserving tribal languages; using curricula and pedagogy that draw from Native communities and genuinely engages tribal elders as scholars; and intentionally working with non-Native teacher candidates to inform them about the complex history of Native Americans so as not to reproduce a culture of trauma, colonization, and assimilation in Native schools.

SCC also seeks to make education more feasible for Native students, many of whom live in poverty. For example, with grant money, SCC is now able to give every student in the program free full tuition and a thousand-dollar stipend for daycare. This not only makes it possible for tribal members to complete their teacher education degree but also demonstrates the deep commitment of the college to bringing the vision and control of Native student education back to the reservation. As one professor at SCC reflected on the history of removing Native American students from their families and communities and training teachers at colleges that did not value tribal culture and values:

> We worked really hard to get teacher education back. We all knew that teacher education was a focal point of our communities. The most significant organizations on these reservations are the school systems; the most vital. If we're not putting Native Americans back into those positions that are being vacated, then we're not doing a service to our communities.

EVERY STEP FORWARD *SEA CON PASO FIRME*: STORIES AND IMAGES OF TEACHING IN CALIFORNIA'S CENTRAL VALLEY

> Being an educator in the Central Valley of California means teaching respect for our environment and the people who keep our community moving. Every student creates their story in the context of this valley, surrounded by surcos, canales, manos callosas, y tierra fertil. We exist in an El Dorado, where grizzlies traveled down the rivers we splash in and bandidos held hideouts in the hills that adorn our drive. The history of this valley is being added to with every step our students take, and it is up to us as educators to equip them so that every step forward sea con paso firme.
>
> —candidate, California State University,
> Fresno's Teacher Credential Program

The quote above was written as part of an innovative assignment in California State University, Fresno's Culturally and Linguistically Sustaining

Pedagogy (CLSP) course wherein teacher candidates were asked to represent in images and words what it means to them to teach in the Central Valley of California. More specifically, candidates were required to create their own original Loteria Card, which is a Mexican game like Bingo. The assignment read as follows:

> Create, develop, or co-construct an **IMAGE** that symbolizes what it means to teach in the Central Valley. The goal is to elevate your perspectives and artistic expression. Use this opportunity to reimagine an educational system that arms diverse cultures, languages, and community talent. Please make sure you have a **FRONT** and **BACK** of a single LOTERIA CARD that represents who YOU are or aspire to be as an educator.

In addition to creating the card itself, candidates were asked to record a short video that shared "what gives life to your work" and to write an accompanying reflection that addresses the question: "How does this Loteria Card represent YOU?"

California's Central Valley has a large immigrant and migrant population, many of whom are first-generation college students, representing culturally and linguistically diverse backgrounds. Though most candidates considered themselves to be Americans, they were deeply influenced by their Mexican roots and the stories, or testimonios, that accompanied their family journeys. The merging and overlapping of these various cultural identities were reflected in the images they chose and the words that accompanied them for this assignment. For example, one candidate replaced the traditional American image of a "teacher's apple" with her favorite fruit, the mango, explaining:

> I made the decision to incorporate an alternative to the traditional teacher's apple in a way that would speak to students from the valley. On my card I drew myself holding a *flor de mango con chamoy y tajin*. Mango has always been my favorite fruit and something that brings back fond memories of my time at my grandpa's *huertas* in Jalisco, but the first time I ever saw it cut open into a *flor* was when my son's grandmother, who is *originaria de Guanajuato*, made me one here in Firebaugh. This served as a bridging for me not only between my culture but also between different Mexican cultures. This is a great example of what *el valle* also serves as, a melting pot for Hispanic cultures and traditions.

Some of the candidates' cards also reflected the struggles they experienced being part of two cultures, which fueled their commitment to being culturally relevant teachers, such as the candidate who chose the image of a butterfly with two wings to represent being bilingual and embracing both Latina and American identities. The wings on her Loteria card were also symbolic of this candidate's desire to "give my students their wings to be confident and successful in their future." As someone who had grown up in the Central Valley herself, she reflected that "What inspired me to create my Loteria card was thinking about the memories and experiences I had from going to school in El Centro Valle." Acknowledging that students in the Central Valley need lots of motivation and connections to succeed due to poverty, lack of help at home, family separations, lack of resources, and parents and children not understanding English, this candidate concludes that "We as teachers need to get through all of that and help the students succeed. It also helps to integrate culture into the classroom, because those students will begin to feel involved and connected to the content. Which will obviously help them learn faster."

What was particularly striking about looking at their Loteria cards and reading their reflections, however, was the obvious pride that candidates felt giving back to the communities that had once nurtured them. As one candidate reflected about the process of designing her card:

The title for my Loteria card is "La Maestra" [The Teacher]. I have come a long way and I love referring to myself as a teacher. My parents speak Spanish, and they proudly tell our family members that I am "la maestra" de mi family. That is the main reason I titled it in Spanish. Another reason I put this as the title was because I signify what it means to teach in the Central Valley. When you enter schools around the valley you tend to see a handful of Hispanic teachers that may come from diverse backgrounds just like their students. I myself am Mexican and I love that I got to return to my community in Kerman that has many Hispanic/Latino students.

Most prominently, candidate's Loteria cards and narratives expressed their commitment to providing their future students with the knowledge and drive to ensure that the next generation will embrace their cultural roots. As one candidate wrote, "As educators, it is our responsibility to equip our students with the knowledge and understanding they will need not only to be successful, but to be able to leave their own mark on this valley.... We are building upon the work that many educators, activists, and laborers have left for us, and our students will be the next generation to add their own mark."

This assignment is one example of how California State University, Fresno's teacher preparation program embeds culturally relevant pedagogy into its curriculum. In the same class, candidates are given another autobiographical assignment in which they are asked to describe their personal relationship to writing and reading, including addressing questions such as: "Who influenced it? What do you remember about 'learning' to speak your language? What have your experiences been in school? At home? In other spaces/communities?" After reflecting on these questions, candidates address the larger questions: "Why is it important to understand your own background and cultural upbringing? How does this affect your teaching practices?" In responding to this assignment and similar ones, many candidates switched between English and Spanish in their written narratives, embracing linguistic pluralism as an asset rather than a deficit. One candidate, for example, wrote:

> Culturally, I struggled a bit as a child to identify with being American or Mexican. I was too brown to be considered American, but my dad was born in California and didn't work in the fields, so I wasn't Mexican enough. Many of my friends at school either had two parents that came from Mexico, *trabajaban en un racho,* and had a house in Mexico, or they had two parents who were born and went to school here. . . . We would hear both Spanish, English, and what my Mexican cousins would call "pocho" Spanish. In addition, every summer my parents would take us to Mexico to visit my mom's family. In Jalisco we would be at the mercado, speaking Spanish with our cousins, counting *pesos en los puestos,* and comparing life between California and Jalisco. Having this mix of Jalisco and Tejano food and customs greatly influenced my culture.

Reflecting upon how this assignment had an impact on the kind of teacher they aspired to become, several candidates felt strongly that they did not want their students to have to feel pulled between two languages and cultures and, in the words of one candidate, "by going on my own cultural journey I am better equipped to help them navigate their own." This candidate further shared:

> Growing up in a predominately Hispanic community I always felt [pressured] to embrace either one of my identities or the other, and my American identity often won. For a portion of my life, I did not really understand how the different aspects that make me who I am—being a woman, being Mexican American, being an older sister—shaped the way that I viewed and experienced the world. By understanding my own cultural background, I am able to better serve my future students. Many facets of my background may be relatable to students who grew up in similar circumstances, or who are struggling with analogous identity struggles. As a future educator, it is of the utmost importance to me that I place my students' individual identities at the forefront of their educational experience. By going on my own cultural journey, I am better equipped to help them navigate their own. By learning how to decipher not only my cultural identity—but also figuring out how I feel about that identity—I hope to be better suited to teach students that may experience similar circumstances and continue to enhance the magnification of multiculturalism.

Another candidate echoed this desire to see her students feel included, writing that "Having a bilingual teacher really helped my transition from a school in Mexico to a U.S. school. . . . Most of all I want my students to feel proud of who they are. I don't want them to become the silent students of the class because they feel like they don't belong."

"YOU CAN'T SIT BEHIND A DESK": VISIBILITY AND BLACK ROLE MODELS AT JACKSON STATE UNIVERSITY

You can't sit behind a desk. You have to be visible and be out in the community.

—Jackson State University teacher education professor

Many of us picture professors as either standing in front of a classroom or sitting behind a desk. Yet one of the hallmarks of MSIs in general, and HBCUs specifically, is a strong commitment to being visible in the community, including building partnerships with local schools and other community-based organizations. This commitment is partially because the majority of HBCU students are drawn from in-state and/or nearby communities and plan to stay and work in those same communities after graduation (Conrad & Gasman, 2015). Almost half of Jackson State University's (JSU) students are local to Mississippi. All aspects of Jackson State's teacher education program reflect this dedication to working with and improving the local community and public schools, from the hiring of its professors to candidate recruitment to service-learning mandates to providing induction support for their graduates to offering ongoing professional development for in-service teachers.

When the current dean of education began at JSU, he believed that having teacher education faculty who were former K–12 teachers and principals was critical to the mission of the teacher education program. According to the dean:

> I don't look to hire professors who are somewhat antiquated or stagnant. Most of my hires have been people who work in K–12.... We have two professors in education leadership who are former principals. In elementary education, our last three hires have been former teachers. So that's the greatest way that we're making a connection, is to really get K–12 people in here.

In addition to hiring faculty who have recent and relevant experience in the K–12 environment, JSU also puts a strong emphasis on recruiting future teacher candidates from schools in the local community. Under the auspices of programs such Teach for Mississippi, representatives from the JSU teacher education program are creating organizations in local middle and high schools that aim to inspire students to become teachers. Through joining these organizations, local high school students get to live on JSU's campus over the summer and experience first-hand the culture of higher education and teacher education. According to the dean, "We feel that in the long run it's going to build that teacher pool that we so badly need." As he further explains, "We do our best here at Jackson State to stay acquainted with the K–12 schools. That was my mission in coming here. I feel we did a great job. Well, when I got here there was a disconnect. What we did right away was that we started connecting with all the K–12 schools."

The dean's commitment to connect with the local schools is also reflected in the teacher education program's early and repeated opportunities for candidates to work in local K–12 classrooms. For example, when asked how professors challenge teacher candidates, one professor responded: "Real life situations, letting the students see that, yes, you have this textbook in front of you and all this theory that's in it, but let's see what's practical. Let's go out into the field and see what really is taking place." Early exposure to real-time classroom teaching provides an opportunity for candidates to see what teaching feels like. It also provides them with a chance to experience what it feels like to serve as a positive role model for Black students and to go beyond the textbook to teach students about cultural pride and resilience, something many of them never experienced in their own education. As one candidate shared with us, "My opinion of an effective teacher is someone that students can look up to. They understand what you must learn in the classroom, but you want to teach them other things outside of the things in the book. You want to teach them lifelong lessons and things they should know in the future."

While CRP is often associated with what we teach (e.g., creating lesson plans and choosing texts that include or reflect diverse cultural histories and experiences), it is also deeply embedded in how we teach. That includes learning how to create a classroom where students feel safe and are treated with respect, and subsequently can be active learners. According to one candidate at JSU:

> The biggest priorities in my class will be respect and safety. I want my students not only to respect themselves and others in the classroom, but to know that I respect them as well and that this is a safe environment for learning and creativity. My main goals for my first year of teaching are to instill core values like respect, impart knowledge that can be used in the outside world as well as the classroom, and to teach my students to be active learners instead of students who are just "good" test takers.

Teacher candidates at JSU are aware that they are role models for students and have a responsibility to create a safe and respectful environment that encourages creativity, critical thinking, and active learning. Candidates we interviewed spoke about the importance of being a positive role model, including the importance of recognizing Black students' assets, supporting their goals and dreams, while holding them to high expectations. These commitments stand in the face of centuries of educational denial, inequality, and marginalization of Black students. Research has found that having even one Black teacher in elementary school not only makes children more likely to graduate from high school, it makes them much more likely to enroll in college as well, and yet, Black people are still only about 7% of the teaching profession (Rosen, 2018). Black men make up just 2% of the teaching profession (Koenig, 2021). National estimates indicate that state public school teachers are "on average 27 percentage points more likely to be white than their students" (Schaeffer, 2021). These statistics—grim under any circumstances—are particularly distressing given that there was a time when Black students were taught almost exclusively by Black teachers who were advocates and active members of their own communities. As Rogers-Ard et al. (2012) note:

> Prior to *Brown v Board of Education*, African American communities created schools, developed teachers and school leaders, and created pathways into Historically Black Colleges and Universities (HBCUs), with notions of service to communities as a component of degree attainment. With the implementation of desegregation, Black schools were closed, Black children were sent to White-led schools, and Black educators lost their jobs. (p. 453)

While we are certainly not arguing against desegregation—as schools with large numbers of Black children were and continue to be under-resourced in comparison to schools with a majority White population—it is important to understand the Black student experience in the United States within a larger historical context to understand teacher education at JSU. According to Rogers-Ard et al. (2012), after the *Brown* decision:

> The commitment of locally run schools to develop socially just, community-minded graduates dissipated with integration as White educators did not share the same commitment, expertise, or familiarity with the community context of racism and poverty that Black students lived in. Formal schooling was no longer seen as a process to learn how to serve and improve local communities, much less become a teacher, partially because there were no longer accessible models of culturally responsive, community-based teachers, and partially because African American students were now required to learn a White-framed curriculum taught by White teachers. (Roders-Ard et al., 2012, p. 454)

JSU is one of many HBCUs that is trying to reclaim its roots in teacher education and help teacher candidates to strategically dismantle barriers to Black students' academic achievement, including challenging racist practices in schools, providing holistic support for students who are struggling, and making sure that all students feel respected and welcome in the classroom. In short, candidates at JSU are faced with undoing centuries of racist practices that framed Black students (and Black families) as culturally deficient and academically inferior. According to research conducted by JSU's dean, for example, in the local middle schools 33% of all the students were one grade or two grades behind, and close to 70% of students were reading below proficient levels. He further notes that "The Yazoo Public Schools were 99.9% African American, but in both elementary schools it was 95% [White] teachers. Their children were attending private schools."

So, while having Black teachers is not a cure-all for Black students, there is ample evidence to support that it can make a huge difference. Indeed, the most common motivation for these candidates to teach was so that they could be effective role models and mentors for Black students—especially Black men students—as these students were not accustomed to seeing Black men in intellectual or leadership positions. One candidate told us: "When I was growing up it was only two males in my elementary school. I didn't have one male that actually taught me. So, I felt there was a need for African American teachers, especially since I was one that was raised in a single parent home." Candidates shared that just seeing a Black man standing in front of the classroom can be a profoundly motivational experience for many Black students. For example, one candidate reflected:

> I feel like I can never say that I'm a teacher and walk into a classroom. This is what generally has happened: I can walk into a classroom, and everything could just shift like everything will just shift to myself or to me. All the students will look, look, and wonder. Like their eyes are sparkling, like who is this person? It's amazing because I've never said a word. All I did was just walk into the classroom. They'll take notice of you in almost every aspect they can manage to think of. They'll ask you questions. How old are you? Where are you from? What are you doing? They'll also consider your body language. The different things that you display to them is what you will be to them.

Candidates at JSU also stressed how important it was to start being a role model and mentor to Black students as early as possible, prompting many candidates to major in elementary education. One candidate remarked:

> I wanted to be somebody's role model. I specifically want to start in elementary school because that's where children start to find themselves and they learn how to act in public and everything else. I want to start right there in the beginning so I can make them go to the right start.

JSU teacher candidates also recognized that they have a responsibility to empower students to be future leaders, as best expressed by one candidate:

> I'm interested in teaching because I'm in a spot to develop America's future. Children are always going to be our future and if we get them and teach them while they're young they will be taking over this country eventually and they're getting into the mindset of I can be a better me if I'm better I could better my

country. So just to be in that position to put them in that mindset and to open their eyes to see that they can change the world is why I want to be a teacher.

Aware of the fact that Black students are disproportionately disciplined when they often just need help or attention, another candidate shared his belief that teachers must have a loving heart:

> You've got to have a loving heart when you're teaching peoples' children. Some of them come from a bad background and school is the only place where they can get someone to show them some attention. So that's why some of them act badly. I want to be a teacher that loves my kids and when I'm teaching them as well help them learn and not one of those teachers that I'm just here for the paycheck.

When asked why he thinks JSU has "the best education program," one candidate replied:

> Because I feel like they understand where we're coming from as far as the classroom. I feel that any other school they'll just tell you like oh well you just need to know this philosopher and what they're talking about. But here they'll really tell you we understand what's going on in the elementary classroom: We'll tell you and we'll be honest with you what's really about to happen.

As a result of this transparency, JSU teacher candidates are less likely to experience what has become known as "practice shock," where new teachers are not fully prepared to deal with many of the complex and less-than-ideal realities of teaching in underserved and underresourced schools. Practice shock is a major reason why many new teachers end up leaving the profession, but it is particularly poignant for teachers of color who are not prepared for the systemic racism they are about to encounter. This racism—which is built into all aspects of schooling from unfair discipline policies to unfair tracking policies to culturally biased testing and assessment policies—not only prevents teachers of color from being a strong advocate for their students, but it can also remind them of their own traumatic experiences in school, leaving them feeling frustrated and powerless (Kohli, 2018).

JSU candidates shared multiple stories about how they came into the classroom with one set of lesson plans and had to shift midway to truly engage their students and teach their strengths rather than their weaknesses. As one candidate recalled:

> I had a student who had ADHD and so he couldn't just sit still. I was up there teaching them the ABCs. So, I had to incorporate dance moves. We did the music chair ABCs and when it stopped everybody sat down. He had a problem, and he couldn't just sit down so I tried to put words to the music to differentiate instruction to help this child out.

Another candidate similarly remembered his first experience in the classroom where he had a mentally challenged student:

> I had never worked with any child that was mentally challenged but it was a great learning experience because it taught me [whether] I wanted to go into Special Education. Yeah, you have to have patience in the classroom already but with them you have to have a lot more patience. You have to kind of give them a little more attention than others. He was a good kid. I enjoyed being there with him.

JSU's candidates typically give their students more attention by spending more time with them outside of the formal classroom.

In fact, JSU teacher candidates are required to do community service during their preparation. These aspects of the program will be discussed more fully in Chapter 4, in which we describe JSU's Call Me Mister Program, and in Chapter 6, where we talk about the ways that servant leadership and community service are embedded in the JSU program. What is important to underscore here is that teacher preparation programs at JSU start with the assumption that teachers can have a profound impact on students' lives and, as such, must be committed to nurturing all aspects of their students' education by teaching both inside and outside the book, and getting out from behind the desk. As one professor at JSU shared with us, this work is urgent: "We're at the point in our lives now [where] we know we don't have time to play games because we know it is crucial that we prepare our students. It's not about us. It's a generational thing. We have to teach them. It's important. You think it's important because you are going to impact the lives of others." A candidate in the program echoed this sentiment, sharing with us: "I'm interested in teaching because I'm in a spot to develop America's future. Children are always going to be our future and if we can get to them and teach them while they're young that they all will be taking over this country eventually and they're getting into the mindset of I can be a better me and if I'm better I could better my country. So just to be in that position to put them in that mindset and to open their eyes to see that they can be the change in the world is why I want to be a teacher."

CULTURALLY RELEVANT PEDAGOGY AS COMMUNITY ANALYSIS

The Community Analysis (CA) Project is an assignment that New Mexico State University (NMSU) professors Jeanette Haynes Writer and Prentice Baptiste (former dean of NMSU's College of Education) use as part of their Multicultural Education course for teacher candidates. From the outset of the class, the professors clarify that this is not a "how to do multicultural education" course but a conceptual, research-based course that will enable candidates to understand what social justice looks like. According to Haynes Writer and Baptiste (2009), "We must provide opportunities for our pre-service teachers to operationalize MCE (multicultural education)" (n.p.). Haynes Writer and Baptiste (2009) believe that "The CA [project] compels pre-service teachers to analyze systemic inequities and inequities in communities, which impact the everyday lives of students" (n.p.). Baptise describes the origins of the assignment as follows:

> Very often in teacher preparation programs around the country the focus is quite centered on the school. We felt that the students [candidates] who matriculate through a teacher preparation program should become knowledgeable about the community in which the students are coming from. Subsequently we felt like part of our preparation of teachers, especially as it fits into the multicultural course, was a twelve-week experience focusing on what is happening in the communities that these students come from. We felt that teachers very often do not live in the community in which these students come from. In terms of teacher preparation, we felt like our teachers should be out in these communities also. (n.p.)

While many MSIs draw teacher candidates from local communities, as a state university, NMSU also has a lot of students who are unfamiliar with the surrounding school districts and neighborhoods. The goal of the CA Project is to create a hands-on learning opportunity, which uses research and reflective practice to prepare preservice teachers to provide equitable and just learning environments for all students. Candidates are required to select a school site but not to go into the school. Instead, preservice teachers must "image themselves as future teachers in their particular school," addressing questions such as, "What are the issues in the community that serve as obstacles for the students? What are the strengths and resources of the community? How is power played out? How can one bridge the school curriculum with the organic knowledge that students bring to school?" Candidates also must construct a "descriptive map" of the school community, including the names of the specific areas, villages, streets, or roads in the community. Candidates use a color and a number code to fill in the map, designating places such as community service agencies, religious/spiritual or political organizations, housing, play areas, business areas, as well as areas where unemployed gather or where there are condemned buildings. Candidates also complete a questionnaire that focuses on attention to issues such as "quality and availability of food and housing, social issues, physical infrastructure viability, and perspectives of residents regarding the community." To answer these questions, candidates consult research journals, websites, and U.S. Census data as a way of expanding preservice teachers' resourcefulness in locating community information and resources.

After candidates spend 12 weeks immersed in their selected communities observing and talking with diverse members of the community, the CA

Project culminates in a critical analysis paper, bringing all the information they have collected and learned together. A key guiding question for this paper is, "What have you learned about the manifestations of race/ethnicity, socio-economic class, gender, sexual orientation, language, ability, and religion in the community?" and "How are power and oppression connected to these diversities displayed or played out in the community?" Candidates are also asked to consider how they might address the most prominent issues they identified in the community through their work with students in the classroom and their caregivers. According to Haynes Writer and Baptise (2009), "This engages the pre-service teachers with MCE [multicultural education] teaching conceptualizations and strategies that purposefully transcend 'food, fun, and festivals' approach as a means to establish and maintain equitable and socially just learning environments for all students" (n.p.).

When asked about the significance of this assignment for culturally relevant pedagogy, Baptise responded:

> We felt like students' preparation to be teachers in various school districts usually did not know what the communities were really like. That is, did they really have a thorough knowledge of how the communities operated that these students came from? The community is a very significant aspect in the education of students, the funds of knowledge, the knowledge in the community. That should be part of the preparation of working with children in schools, and, of course, the preparation of teachers. Why do we think community analysis is important? Very often in teacher preparation programs around the country the focus is quite centered on the school. Our [candidates] perhaps don't get the significance that the community plays in the education of students. We felt that the [candidates] who matriculate through a teacher preparation program should become knowledgeable about the community in which the students are coming from. We felt that teachers very often do not live in the community in which these students come from. In terms of teacher preparation, we felt like our teachers should be out in these communities also. We wanted them to go and observe, to reflect on their observations, and to correlate that with the readings we had for them to do.

According to Baptise, candidates "are reluctant to want to go into communities, especially communities that they may not be very familiar with. At the beginning they say, 'Why do I have to do this?'" At the end of the project, however, Baptise found that many students were inspired by what they had seen:

> Many students felt like there was something they learned that they gained knowledge that they didn't realize was out there that was experiential, practical knowledge, and how it related to what they were reading. They began to realize

that some schools really had an advantage over other schools, in terms of which community they were located in. There were inequities in terms of housing, inequities regarding resources. As an example, compare one elementary school that had a PTO [parent teacher organization] and through fundraising raised something like $25,000 for their students, for their teachers to be able to utilize. While another school, putting on the same kind of fundraising, reaching out to the community only raised about $1,600. So, they realized what a discrepancy that is. They began to realize what was going on in society, what was going on in education in terms of where the inequities really existed to a great extent. It's one of those kinds of learnings that you consider to be a deep learning. You may forget what you've read, but if you really have that type of experience it stays with you. It comes up when you are doing your student teaching and when you go out teaching in other schools. The value of that experience should always be a part of my course. What you know is what you've been allowed to know. And that's how you control people.

The research presented in this chapter provides numerous examples of what CRP looks like in teacher education across diverse contexts and institutions. CRP can show up in different ways. For example, in Stone Child College, CRP was the basis for the organization and sequencing of the entire program around the Cree Medicine Wheel. At California State University, Fresno, CRP was embodied in an assignment that prompted candidates to do deep and multifaceted reflection on how their own cultural identities and experiences influence their persona as future teachers. At Jackson State University, CRP was evident in how teachers were being prepared to approach future students from an asset-based perspective, which stands in stark contrast to how Black students are typically treated in educational settings. At New Mexico State University, CRP became part of a research assignment to get to know the surrounding community.

While CRP looks different at various institutions, a common thread is that it requires a real commitment to addresses issues of educational equity, as well as challenging the status quo of White power and privilege. To quote Petchauer and Mawhinney (2017) once again, this means much more than simply increasing diversity in the teacher's lounge; we need to look carefully at the design and structure of teacher education across the entire program. While ideally teacher education programs will hire and support faculty from diverse cultures and backgrounds and draw a greater pool of candidates from local communities who are deeply invested in the students they teach, CRP is not something that should be reserved for teachers and candidates of color. Our research suggests that some MSIs are leading the way in creating teacher education programs that are culturally relevant across all coursework and classroom practice, and responsive to the complex needs and experiences of specific and intersectional student populations.

CHAPTER 4

"Belonging"
Faculty Support and Cohort Models in MSI Teacher Education Programs

> Central to the shared missions of MSIs is a widely shared assumption about post-secondary education: not only can all students succeed, but faculty, staff, students, and surrounding communities share an obligation to see that all students are successful.... many minority students choose MSIs because they believe they will have a sense of belonging at college without sacrificing their cultural identity or educational goals. (Conrad & Gasman, 2015, p. 23)

As we have shared, in addition to being students of color, most teacher candidates at MSIs are also from first-generation, low-income communities, and many more are English language learners (ELLs), immigrants, or migrants. These students are typically not raised with the expectation that they will go to college, and many come from secondary school environments where they were not encouraged or supported to pursue college aspirations. Those who can successfully enroll in higher education programs often arrive having limited access to college preparatory courses and counseling and lack much needed financial literacy. Moreover, while MSIs tend to attract students from local communities, there are still a significant proportion of students who are leaving their homes and communities, including reservations, for the first time. They miss and worry about their families, including parents who depend upon them for extra income and younger siblings who they fear may not have the same opportunities. As they explore the campuses where they will spend the next years of their lives, they often don't know how to navigate college and don't know who to trust. They are looking for more than just academic guidance; they need to find new culturally sensitive, flexible, and holistic support systems. A hallmark of MSIs is intentional hiring of nurturing student-centered faculty, the majority of whom are also people of color from minoritized and underserved backgrounds. Along with academic success, MSI faculty prioritize genuine student engagement, belonging, and care. In contrast to many institutions of higher education, which privilege and reward faculty research over teaching, MSIs are more commonly teaching institutions. While this does not mean that MSI faculty are not interested in research, their number one priority is their students, which in turn is connected to empowering underserved communities and opening new pathways for educational equity. In his study of the motivations and paths to becoming an MSI faculty member, Blake (2018) found that values such as benefiting others, community uplift, and education for social change were instrumental in the hiring of MSI faculty. Blake suggests that "MSIs appear to attract community-oriented individuals to their faculty positions" and concluded that "the aspiration to become a professor was linked to helping MSIs serve marginalized communities" (p. 14). In their own extensive research of MSIs across the nation, Gasman and Conrad (2013) concur, underscoring that:

> MSIs have a record of success with underserved and often underprepared students in part because they believe that the challenges that many of their students face are not due to a lack of capabilities but rather to a lack of opportunities. Why does this belief matter? By believing in every student and expecting them to succeed, MSIs create environments where students who have had little success in school in the past find hope, motivation, and support. (p. 18)

Thus, rather than weed students out, MSIs exist to build students up. MSIs distinguish themselves as institutions where, with the right support, opportunities, and encouragement, all students can succeed. They also go to great lengths to make students feel like they belong there, something that more privileged students at PWIs might take for granted. Some of the ways in which MSIs accomplish this sense of belonging are discussed in this chapter, including (1) creating a family-like atmosphere; (2) hiring faculty members who care deeply about student success, combining high expectations with high levels of support; and (3) using cohort models.

LIKE FAMILY

A hallmark of MSIs is that faculty and students work together in a manner like that of a family. According to Gasman and Nguyen's (2019) study of STEM majors at HBCUs, *Making Black Scientists*:

> As students at the HBCUs in this study were viewed as family, faculty members were protective and held them accountable on a daily basis. The very notion of family means offering unwavering support while having high expectations. The combination of the two leads to success for students who want to be both held accountable and nurtured in their learning environments. (p. 177)

Likewise, Petchauer and Mawhinney (2017) describe the form of mentoring at MSIs as "other parenting," in which faculty members take on familial responsibilities (p. 390). Indeed, the candidates in the teacher education programs we visited often used the phrase "like family" when talking about both their professors and their peers. Comments such as "It feels like home," and "It feels like a family to be honest" were common ways that candidates described their experiences in their programs. Candidates also made a special point to recognize the personalized support they received from their professors, many of whom became fictive kin, such as the candidate at California State University, Fresno, who told us of her program co-directors, "They're like our mom and our dad." Another candidate remarked similarly about his program supervisor, emphasizing that "We share the same background. We both came from Mexico and he's really a humble guy. He's really down to earth. He appeals to every learning style even for us as students. He really cares for each individual student. . . . He's Pepe[1] to everybody." When asked why it makes a difference to have a caring professor from a similar background, the candidate answered, "Because we always look at what they've achieved and where they're coming from. It just gives us the [idea] of we can get there too."

When speaking about the relationship between candidates and program supervisors, one faculty member at California State University, Fresno, emphasized that "They are like family. There's no end, there's no limit to the mentoring that students get. We're very mindful of the fact that we don't want to be top down. We don't want to come in with a deficit lens." As MSI faculty are frequently drawn from the local community, some candidates also made a point of sharing with us that faculty knew their parents and families: "They know you, they've known your family and they know, oh yeah, you look like your mom or your dad. They've just kind of been here so long."

"NOT JUST A NUMBER": PERSONALIZED AND HOLISTIC FACULTY CARE

When asked what they think makes a good teacher, candidates were quick to respond: "caring." One candidate from New Mexico State University concluded: "It's a person that really cares about their students in different areas, not just academics like mathematics or being able to answer a question on a test. That is one part, but in addition to that is who they are, how they connect, who the family is, how can they get close to you to support you as a human being. So that to me is what a good teacher is, a caring person." Some candidates who we met with began their journey at other schools and ultimately chose to enroll in an MSI precisely because, as one candidate shared, "The teachers seem like they really care and you can talk to them and it was just a very different experience for me, being here at NMSU so I ended up just staying."

MSI faculty demonstrated their care for candidates in multiple ways. While there is no doubt that the faculty members we met with had high expectations for candidates (which is discussed in more detail later in this chapter), they also knew that candidates struggled with competing priorities such as work and school or having to take care of family members. With the goal of student success, faculty thus sought to accommodate these students rather than penalize them. As one faculty member at California State University, Fresno, underscored, "Students are in some ways really struggling. We have a lot of food insecure students. We have a lot of students who have children before entering college. We have students with significant issues on their plate and a lot of responsibility. They're not the kind of college students who have someone paying for them to go to school for four years and [can just] focus on being students. They are students who are working their way through and who often have a job and are struggling to get childcare, and in some cases choosing between the textbook and a meal."

Similarly, a candidate at Stone Child College shared, "If one of our family members gets sick or gets hurt, we all take care of each other. The faculty understand if we must miss days because of things like that. If you're missing it, they give you a chance to make it up. They don't try to ride you about it." Another candidate shared that "That's the one thing that faculty will understand. If you have to leave in emergencies and stuff like that. I'm able to talk to the teachers about the situations instead of being afraid or always being docked on points or grades or anything." This student further reflected that "Sometimes days I missed class due to something else, I can come in and get the notes from them or they can email me the notes. I can come in and make up an assignment any time and they'll just have me back there in the conference room or the lunchroom and make up tests back there. The faculty and teachers are here to help you be successful."

Candidates also emphasized that faculty went to great lengths to make them feel like they belonged in the program even when they were struggling academically. One candidate shared:

> With the professors, they make you feel like you belong here. They're there to help. If you ever need extra help afterwards or if you don't grasp a subject very well. Our physics teacher, he would stay after class and he would say I know that physics isn't the best or the easiest subject to comprehend, if you have any questions just come down, let me know, and I'll explain to you, or I can even demonstrate for you how this concept works.

Candidates thus took advantage of repeated opportunities to have a faculty member's personalized attention, such as the candidate who emphasized, "You're not just a number, and you get one-on-one relations with your teacher." One program director confirmed this, stating that "It's more important that we be out of our offices with the students. We've got plenty of work to do too but we take this time out to be with them so that we're accessible." Another professor told us of the candidates in her program: "I think in all departments across the campus they feel like they can talk to the professors. We have that open door policy. They can come in and just sit down and talk with us. It's one of the things that makes us feel like a family unit. . . . we have an open-door policy, and we try to nurture our students to some small degree to help them along the way."

This connection with faculty was reinforced by smaller class sizes where they felt seen and by faculty's widespread respect for candidate's individuality and diversity. One candidate told us, "The classes are a good size where we're all able to express or to talk in classes and not just be in the back and just sit there." Another candidate noted that the faculty encouraged her to be her authentic self: "Just coming in here and being who I am, not trying to be anybody else or try to please anybody else. There's a sense of comfortability here and a sense of knowing people, [having] a personal relationship with people."

It is also significant that faculty support did not stop when students left the classroom or campus. As one faculty member told us, "I run into students in the community all the time who will talk about something that changed their lives. I just feel like there's a recognition of the effort to make this more of a community of practice rather than this top-down infrastructure of me being the sage or the person in charge." This same faculty member shared, "I give students my number and they will call me. They will email me if they have issues that are sometimes even unrelated to the course work." The candidates we met with had many examples of times when faculty members went above and beyond for them. One candidate at Jackson State University, for example, described his relationship with the director of his program in the following way:

> He is one of the people who goes beyond his role. I can talk to him about anything, even if it is not school. Like one time I needed help with a flat tire, he was there. There are also times I call him, and he's been able to come and help me out if I need advice dealing with relationships or family problems. He'll listen and give me advice. He's really like a big brother or father or uncle to everybody.

When asked if he saw himself as a father figure to the students in the program, the director responded, "I do. I joke about it sometimes. Sometimes they get a little more attention than my nine-year old does, at least academically. I do kind of see myself as a father figure and again what I want to do is just help them make good decisions so that they can be the best that they can be in what they're doing."

While some might see this level of faculty involvement as coddling students, it reinforces a candidate's sense of personal investment and accountability. As one candidate at Jackson State University told us, "We have some pretty good advisory here. They give you the plan, but it's left up to you to follow it. They can't just hold our hand, but they give us good guidance. They give us a lot of resources. You just must have the discipline to use it." A candidate at Stone Child College similarly remarked, "You can't fail here. If you're going to fail here the only person that's going to make you fail is yourself. The faculty is here to help you succeed and learn."

That said, forging these kinds of relationships with their students is not always easy for MSI professors, many of whom teach up to five classes a semester and are working with students who face a lot of challenges to academic success. For example, as one professor at Jackson State shared:

> The thing that's most challenging would probably be just really kind of serving as a counselor for 15 young Black men ranging from 18 to 21 years of age. So, any time you're dealing with a group of young people at that age you're going to have some unique situations that come up. My challenge is day in and day out just really trying to maintain contact with them and make sure that they're doing the things that they're supposed to do and that they're making good decisions. When they have problems or issues that come up, they usually show up at my door to talk to me. The challenge is basically trying to balance that.

This same professor, however, recognizes that he represents one of the few Black men these students have seen in positions of academic power, further noting that "I'm a teacher role model and I'm also a Black role model. So, it's important for our students to be able to walk into the classroom and see people that look like them." As Petchauer and Mawhinney (2017) suggest, "MSIs also create comprehensive and nurturing environments that advocate for academic development connected to racial self-development" (p. 3). For many students at MSIs, this is the first time they have teachers from similar racial and cultural backgrounds. While MSI faculty seek to create and model a familiar, caring, and high support environment for teacher candidates, they also strategically seek to create opportunities for candidates to support each other. One way this is accomplished is through peer leadership and the use of cohort models.

PEER LEADERSHIP AND SUPPORT: MSI COHORT MODELS

Many MSIs also use cohort models where students become invested in each other's success rather than the more isolated and competitive atmosphere that is typical of higher education. For example, it is common for students at

MSIs to be part of a cohort wherein students take classes and study together, carpool together, and sometimes even live together throughout their entire undergraduate or graduate education (Conrad & Gasman, 2015; Gasman & Nguyen, 2019). For many candidates being part of a cohort where their peers have their backs can literally be the difference between success and dropping out. Gasman and Nguyen (2019) note that an added benefit of the cohort model is that it encourages peer leadership and allows struggling students to recognize and aspire to the success of those who came before them. Rather than a culture of competition that permeates most institutions of higher education then, the candidates at the MSIs we spoke with were quick to recognize the success of their peers and to express gratitude for their support and encouragement. For example, a candidate in Jackson State's teacher education program shared:

> We're there for each other when we need it. We are all in the same class and if I'm struggling with something they'll help me out. If I know something that they're struggling with, I'll be there to help them out. As we go through the program, we are getting closer, and we learn from each other on how to deal with each other and help each other out.

Historically, cohort models are not exclusive to MSIs and have been found to be a successful strategy for teacher education generally, dating back to one of the earliest teacher education cohort models, the Holmes Program. In *Tomorrow's Schools of Education* (1995), faculty members involved with the Holmes Program underscored the importance of creating small learning communities and mutually supporting networks for teacher candidates, underscoring that teacher candidates should be part of a cohort and mutually supportive network that endures throughout their professional careers.

In their own research on cohort models in preservice teacher preparation, Dinsmore and Wenger (2006) concurred, finding that "Students involved in positive relationships in learning communities spend more time studying together and learning from each other," and that participating in cohorts lead to students forming their own supportive peer groups, becoming more actively involved in cooperative learning and increasing their knowledge of teaching (p. 60). According to Bullough et al. (2001), cohorts also relieve a lot of the pressures beginning teachers face and "The more difficult the challenges and the more personal the issues, the more important became the support of students within the cohort" (pp. 100–101). When strategically designed and implemented, the authors concluded that "The cohort organization . . . opens up possibilities unavailable under other more traditional, individualistic, models of teacher education, models which ignore community building" (pp. 103–107). At the same time, however, the authors warn that "Positive cohort learning experiences do not just happen as a matter of good luck, a happy placement, and of spending prolonged time with other teacher education students." They underscore that "Those responsible for teaching within them must attend carefully to build a culture that supports and sustains effective group problem solving" (p. 103).

Two of the strongest and most structured cohort models we found at MSIs were at Jackson State University, where candidates had the option of joining the Call Me MISTER program, and at California State University, Fresno, where candidates had the option of joining the California Mini Corps program (described briefly in the Preface and in Chapter 2). In the remainder of this chapter, we take a closer look at these two programs and why they are so effective.

MY BROTHER'S KEEPER: COHORTS AND CALL ME MISTER AT JACKSON STATE UNIVERSITY

> One of the things that I really want to come out of this is the idea that I'm my brother's keeper. That's actually one of the basic tenets of the program. I would like the MISTERs to basically say that. They realize that they have a responsibility, and their responsibility is not just to themselves but it's to their brothers that are going through the Call Me MISTER program.
>
> —Director of the Call Me MISTER program at Jackson State University

Call Me MISTER (CMM) was developed to attract more Black men into teaching. CMM teacher candidates receive tuition assistance, professional development opportunities, testing workshops, and academic and social mentoring provided by a program coordinator and faculty coach. In exchange, these students commit to teaching for one year in Mississippi public schools for each year that they receive financial assistance. CMM candidates are recruited in cohorts of at least five people, beginning in their first year. They live together on campus in a common residence and take most of their classes together.

It is important to note that CMM is not a teacher education program. The candidates still need to get accepted into the university and pass all the required courses, exams, and certification requirements as regular teacher candidates. It is also important to mention that the CMM program, unlike many other cohort programs (such as Teach for America), does not cherry-pick candidates. As some of the founding CMM faculty and staff explain, "In our program student participants are largely, but not exclusively, selected from underserved, socioeconomically disadvantaged and educationally at-risk communities" (Jones et al., 2019, p. 56). The fact that the program does not cater to the highest achieving students (as based on traditional measures like GPAs and test scores) is reflective of a strong belief that every student has equal potential to succeed if given the right opportunities and support. As the CMM director at JSU explained to us:

> If you look at our MISTERS at Jackson State, we have students that came in on Presidential Scholarships, but we also have students that came in taking remedial courses. What we've done is we've selected them, and we've grouped them all together and we're hoping that through that support system with them going through classes as a cohort and with us providing them with extra support that they're going to ensure that all of them can make it.

This belief that all students have the same potential is reflected in CMM's recruitment model. In addition to typical teacher candidate recruitment sites such as high school and college career fairs the program takes advantage of nontraditional sites and networks such as local barber shops, churches, fraternities, and boy's clubs. According to Holton and Joseph (2019), who have written extensively about the CMM model, "The program places a high premium on networking within local communities to help the CMM recruit stay connected to their story. The program depends on the culture of the very community in which a CMM candidate is rooted" (p. 62). In fact, the current MISTERS at JSU who we met with were intricately involved in recruiting the next cohort and were asked to participate in the interview process because, according to the program director, "We want to make sure that they feel like they have ownership in this program, because this is their program." As such, everyone gets an equal vote as to who is selected into the program.

Once they are accepted into CMM, the program does everything possible to help students reach their goals, often under challenging circumstances. For many African American men college students, interrelated challenges include inadequate precollege preparation, lack of funding and financial capital, anxiety about high-stakes testing, lack of self-confidence, poor understanding about course sequencing and credits needed to graduate, and imposter syndrome (Gist, 2016; Hollins, 2015; Kohli, 2018). CMM, however, does not penalize or isolate students who faced these challenges. Put most clearly by one professor in the program, "We've had instances where students haven't met the GPA requirements. We don't just get rid of students. We don't throw people away." According to one candidate in the program, "You don't have as much stigma attached to you. You can be the smartest or the dumbest and everybody knows one another. That's just kind of how Jackson State is. So, you know everybody. If you don't know their name, you know their faces." Another candidate shared, "Call Me MISTER program, it's a strong brotherhood. I feel like they always have my back." When asked about his relationship with the other men in CMM, another candidate also conveyed a strong family-like relationship among the cohort:

"We're there for each other when we need it. We are all in the same class and if I'm struggling with something they'll help me out. If I know something that they're struggling with, I'll be there to help them out. As we go through the program, we are getting closer, and we are learning from each other on how to help each other out."

Many of the candidates we talked to in the JSU Call Me MISTER Program used the word "brother" to describe their relationship with fellow cohort members. This is part of the formal design of the program, which uses the tagline *You're my Brother's Keeper*, but also something that the candidates clearly took to heart. For example, when asked directly what it means to call his cohort members brothers, one candidate described it as "being individuals under an umbrella." This brotherhood, however, doesn't always happen instantly. According to one candidate we spoke with during his first year in the program, he wasn't focusing on "his brothers" because "I was about self-development and getting myself through the program, make myself seen so that I can continue to progress." Now in his second year, he explained:

> At this point I've come to learn and grow. I'm really taking steps to be more responsible like talking with them more and hanging out and really getting to know these other people in the program so that they're not other people. We're friends, friends, associates, and even as you come along, we're brothers.

Moreover, with the support of being in a cohort like CMM also comes a commitment to keeping each other motivated and accountable. As one candidate explained, "At Jackson State if I don't go to class, I have four or five people calling me: 'Why are you not in class? Where are you at? Do you got this homework done?'" Clearly, this support comes with high expectations. As one candidate remarked of being part of CMM, "It's a community, a nurturing community, with high expectations." These expectations help candidates do their best work but also teach them something important about their role once they are teachers and will need to model this for their own students. As one professor told us, having high expectations and high support is especially important for future teachers to learn, because one day they will be making decisions about the lives of the children in their own classrooms: "Again, the idea is that we don't want them throwing their students away when they go into the K–12 classroom."

As such, when JSU teacher candidates are struggling academically, the goal is neither to fail them or to push them through anyway. Candidates are held to high standards but also receive high support. Sometimes this support means owning up to the fact that a student is falling behind and learning to ask members of your cohort to help. According to the program director, "We put everybody's grades on the board, on the whiteboard. Yes, and we sit and talk about what the problem is. We want them to know whether their brothers are struggling so again they can be there to help them, or if they're not going to class, they need to make sure that they're getting there. That's the whole idea of them being in a cohort and going through it together." CMM thus embeds a strong focus on personal accountability and transparency. As the program director further explained:

> My philosophy is I'm not here to get you out of trouble. I'm here to help you make good decisions. Whatever it is that you have to deal with I'm here to talk to you about it and help, try to help lead you to the responsible decision. But again, at the end of the day you're a grown-up and it's your decision to make and you're going to determine how you handle it. I'm going to advise you but it's your decision ultimately.

MISTERS are encouraged to see their struggles and challenges as opportunities for learning and resilience, as well as to motivate others to excel. When asked about the program's fundamental mission, for example, the program director replied, "Like I said, we have MISTERs that came in on academic probation. We have MISTERs that came in at the top of their class. And they're all kind of going through this experience together." In this respect, CMM encourages all students to believe in themselves and to foster the self-confidence and self-discipline they need to be leaders and advocates for equity inside and outside the classroom.

The candidates we spoke with uniformly agreed that the program was unique in that they received a lot of support but were expected to put the work in too. As one candidate shared about his relationship to the program director:

> Whatever we need him to be, he's there for us and he also helps us with our schoolwork whenever we need it. When we do a paper and we're not sure about something, we can always email him the paper and he'll proofread it and he'll tell us you've got these mistakes and you need to go back and look over this. When I struggled in math, he asked me when I was free and set me up with a math tutor and told me to make sure I'm there. If we have an event coming up, he'll email us to tell us about our event, what we need to do, what we need to wear and what time we can meet up if we need to carpool with classmates.

When asked how he would describe CMM to his friends interested in teaching, one candidate replied, "I tell them if you're in the Call Me MISTER program you have support systems and you're not just going through it on your own. You'll have help until you graduate and after you graduate." In Chapter 6 we discuss how CMM has a distinctive, integrated, and centralized model of servant leadership and community service, which is connected to the cohort model in that all members of the CMM cohort are expected to serve as ambassadors to the communities in which they live, study, and teach. According to JSU's dean of education, the hope is that MISTERS will inspire other Black boys and men to pursue their dreams and goals, understanding that they do not have to do it alone: "We want them to really be able to get out and tell their stories. These guys have really unique stories."

"THEY WERE US": COHORTS AND THE MINI CORPS PROGRAM AT CALIFORNIA STATE UNIVERSITY, FRESNO

The Department of Migrant Services created the California Mini Corps Program (CMC) in 1967; it was patterned after the Peace Corps. The program engages college students from migrant backgrounds as teacher assistants, tutors, translators, and liaisons to migrant children and their families from local K–12 schools. While not a teacher education program, one of its primary goals is to "develop a cadre of future bilingual-bicultural, credentialed teachers that will be better equipped to work with migrant students." Today, approximately 600 Mini Corps members enrolled in colleges across the state tutor 15,000 migrant students—all of whom were either low-income Latinx or Asian American students. As with Call Me MISTER, CMC tutors are required to take all the same coursework, tests, and credentialing requirements as regular students in California State University, Fresno's teacher education program.

There are some significant advantages to being in the CMC program, however. One is that CMC members get exponentially more time to practice and observe in authentic classrooms before becoming teachers themselves. CMC members also have academic supervisors who themselves came from migrant backgrounds. CMC members have extra opportunities to take part in educational workshops and participate in community service activities that enrich the scope and depth of their pathways to becoming culturally responsive teachers. Another benefit of CMC is that it gives candidates a chance to mutually discuss their experiences in the classroom, providing opportunities for peer leadership. As one candidate explained, "We share ideas such as this is working with my classroom. This didn't work out for me."

Perhaps most importantly, CMC members also get a built-in support system by being part of a cohort program. As one CMC candidate explained, "You really get to know your peers and it's amazing because we always talk about the classes we're taking. We kind of help each other out. Sometimes we can't afford our books [and someone will say] 'oh hey I have this book. Do you want it?' I am the first in my family to get this far in education, so I had no guidance. But with everyone here helping you with finding those classes and those resources, you succeed." As with teacher education candidates in other MSIs we visited, CMC members often described the program as a second family. In the words of one candidate:

> We support one another. We're in the credential, the second phase together. How are you doing? Oh, well, I'm struggling. You can do it because we already know each other. We already know that we both want to become teachers regardless of all the obstacles that we're going to face. You can do it. This is how I did it or this is what helped me complete the assignment or complete this within the school environment. That's the way I see motivating each other. You can do it. We're struggling a little, but you're going to become a great teacher. I've seen you. I've observed you. You can do it, and that's the way that we motivate each other by helping each other and by supporting each other.

Another candidate reflected on her overall experience in the program:

> I feel really blessed to be in the Mini Corps Program. I never thought I would have experienced everything that I experienced and supported. They help guide us, and more than anything, being in a group with students who are passionate, who want to become teachers, that's the way that we get motivated. We share ideas . . . this is working with my classroom, but this didn't work out for me. More than anything you have that strong base that helps support you and just keeps you going. Keep going regardless of what's going to be in your way, and that's the way that I see it.

This kind of added support and feeling of belonging is especially important because very few migrant students enroll in higher education. Migrant children are, in fact, among the most vulnerable of all students as they not only come from low-income backgrounds, grapple with English language fluency, and work in the fields alongside their parents after school and on weekends, but they move and change schools as many as four times year. This creates problems with transferring credits and leaves many students feeling like outsiders struggling to make new friends and get acclimated to new school rules and teachers. Many migrant students are put in special education and are subject to bullying. As a result, migrant children are likely to drop out of school, and if they do get to go to college, it is usually because of the added support they get through the CMC Program. Indeed, many of the teacher candidates in the CMC program joined because they were supported by a CMC member when they were in school and were eager to give back. These memories were fresh in their minds. One candidate, for example, shared with us:

> When I was in 6th Grade, I had a Mini-Corps tutor in my classroom, and I wasn't aware that she was a Mini-Corps tutor. I was in the Migrant Program, and she would come in every day and help us. She would help a small group

of migrant students with math, and I just thought it was a college student doing some community service. And I remember, this is what I like about this program. Aside from the academics, the Mini-Corps tutors, there's something about it, just something special. I remember that we had a pizza party, and I didn't bring money that day but we each had to pay for part of our pizza so we could get to participate in the party. She went out to her car (and as a college student now I know that sometimes it is kind of hard on the pocket) and she brought in what she had. She paid for me so I could participate in that party.

This candidate, who later joined CMC himself, further emphasized that:

It's something different about Mini Corps tutors. I saw from her that she wasn't there just to teach us, but she was there to create that rapport, to create that bond. And that's what I hope to accomplish with all my students. I don't want them to feel that it's just that I'm just there, that I don't care about them, that I'm just there to drill them with academics. I want them to know that that's what teachers are there for. We're there because we care about them. We want them to learn because we care about them, and we want them to grow up and be someone.

Many other CMC candidates we met with had similar stories about how they were supported by a CMC tutor in their own education and joined the program as a way of giving back. For example, one candidate told us:

Once I got into Mini-Corps and I really got to work with students, I really started to like it a lot and liked being a role model for these kids. Growing up, I'm the oldest, so when I needed help or something my parents couldn't really help me because they didn't know the language. They didn't know English. So, I was on my own. With Mini-Corps, it's really given me the opportunity to work one on one with students and be that role model for them and really be that help that they might not necessarily have at home.

We also noted that many candidates joined the CMC program because a sibling or classmate had been part of it: "It's a different feeling. I feel like I belong here, I want to say. And since I had family here, my first year, it was the last year of one of my sisters, and I felt like I belonged here because I got to meet her friends. And then I had my friends from high school too. You just feel like you connect automatically and that you belong with the people here." The momentum of being part of a cohort program not only greatly enhanced the sense of belonging but also helped candidates stay motivated, such as the candidate who told us, "More than anything, being in a group with students who are passionate, who want to become teachers, that's the way that we get motivated," or the candidate who shared, "More than anything you have that strong base that helps support you and just keeps going.

Keep going regardless of what's going to be in your way, and that's the way that I see it."

Another unique aspect of the program is that CMC tutors are themselves mentored and supervised by faculty members who also come from migrant backgrounds, thus creating a full circle. Candidates were quick to express their gratitude for the ongoing mentoring and support they received from faculty, such as the candidate who shared, "I feel really blessed to be in the Mini Corps Program. I never thought I would have experienced everything that I experienced and the support. They help guide us." Another candidate agreed: "It makes you feel good to know that you can always have backup of peers or our supervisors." Candidates were also inspired by seeing what former CMC members had accomplished. According to one candidate:

> Even the former Mini Corps, they're now principals and vice principals. You're like, wow. If they were able to become that and they were capable of doing and being in the position that they are, that gives us more motivation that we can do it too because we experienced and faced similar struggles. They were us. That's our motivation.

As we discussed in the previous chapters, the early educational experiences of students of color can be a primary factor in whether they decide to become teachers. Some want to be the teacher they never had, while others want to emulate the teacher that changed their lives. In either case, having faculty that not only look like them but reach out to them like family, provide for them inside and outside the classroom, and see their potential regardless of how much they are struggling is a defining factor in their success. Again, we want to emphasize that this is not the same thing as pushing them through the program with no accountability. In many ways it is just the opposite. Students are given multiple chances as signs of encouragement and respect, but they are ultimately responsible for their decisions and fulfilling their commitment to the program and to becoming teachers.

Moreover, though not all teacher education programs at MSIs use cohort models, the examples we have provided suggest that when well designed and supervised, these models can provide candidates with much needed support and motivation as well as opportunities for peer learning and leadership. When one is part of a race or culture that has faced repeated educational discrimination and discouragement, finding and belonging in a community where your culture is embraced is a powerful experience. In the next chapter we look more closely at how teacher candidates at MSIs are redefining the student teaching model, creating opportunities for candidates to work in schools from the outset of their program with multiple levels of support from faculty and classroom-based mentor teachers working collaboratively.

CHAPTER 5

"Homegrown"
Teacher Residencies and University–School Partnerships

Jordon and Adriana are both candidates in California State University, Fresno's teacher credential program and are also participating in the university's Rural Teacher Residency Program. From the outset of the program, they spend 4 days a week working on-site at a school in a rural school district. This is especially convenient and meaningful for them because they both grew up in and currently live in the neighborhood where they are teaching. In fact, they both attended the same schools that they are now working in, and Jordon's daughter currently attends the same elementary school where she is teaching. One of the extraordinary aspects of this program is that instead of commuting back to the university for their coursework, their professors come to them, teaching in a dedicated classroom space on-site in their community. The alternative would be for Jordon and Adriana to drive up to 75 miles to the university and back each day. According to Jordon, "We can stay with our mentor teachers until 3:15 pm, pretty much until they leave. We'll go home and grab something to eat and then go to our class. It's really convenient that everything is just right here. I feel like this program is a blessing for teachers who really want to work in these communities."

The faculty director of California State University, Fresno's Rural Residency Program agrees, explaining: "It looks so different when candidates have an invested purpose for being in the particular program that they're in. They've really chosen to be a part of the program because they are community members." She said that prior to the Residency Program, candidates in the outlying districts felt they were "never invited to the table" simply because they didn't have the time to commute or access to transportation. By contrast, in the Rural Residency Program, candidates are highly valued members of the community. When asked how they would describe the Rural Residency Program to a prospective teacher candidate, for example, Adriana responded:

> As a person who grew up going to school in the Central Valley, I realized through the program how much the students appreciate representation in the

classroom and seeing someone who is going to care about them as an individual. I feel lucky to be able to give that to them. I just realize the importance of having someone in the classroom of similar background experiences and similar cultural identities and that is able to speak languages that they speak to really be able to help them feel comfortable in the classroom setting.

Jordon added that:

I would say that you definitely have to be someone who is very patient and very understanding because a lot of these students come from low-income households. A lot of teachers start in these rural areas but then they leave. You really have to be passionate about working with these diverse cultures and just in this area in general. This is where I want to be. This is where I want to teach.

Jordon and Adriana are not alone in their desire to give back to the communities they came from. According to another candidate in their residency program:

I specifically wanted to work with students in the rural areas, because that's where I grew up. To be able to give back to the communities that have given me so much would be a dream come true. My journey to become a teacher has been long, but things could not have worked out more perfectly. To be in a credential program designed for aspiring teachers to work in rural areas is like a dream turned reality. I can't wait to have my own classroom of students from rural areas.

Another candidate noted similarly how being able to "relate" to the students strengthened her interest in and commitment to teaching in rural districts: "Teachers from rural schools play an important role in their students' lives. I know this firsthand because I am from the rural areas. I can relate to these students. I am excited to become a teacher and I know I am going to inspire many students."

According to the deputy superintendent at the Fresno County Superintendent of Schools, who was one of the founders of California State University, Fresno's Rural Residency Program, the goal of hiring teachers who grew up in and live in the district was a driving force in creating the program in the first place: "What was happening in those rural districts was that by the time those districts would be needing to hire teachers for the following year, the larger districts in Fresno County would pretty much end up hiring all of the candidates right out of Fresno State as soon as they had graduated. Even before they finished their final student teaching." Determined to grow a pipeline of teachers living in rural communities and committed to working in rural schools, the deputy superintendent approached California State University, Fresno, about creating the Rural Residency Program, recalling that:

> The staff at Fresno State were just ecstatic to get this going. As soon as we mentioned it, they were like 'Can we start tomorrow?' Everybody was on board from Day One. Once Fresno State agreed to do it, I proposed the idea to the four superintendents, and they really just couldn't believe that we were thinking of them, and they couldn't believe that for once in the history of their districts and the history of their communities Fresno State would dedicate resources and money into their four small districts in order to annually create an intentional recruitment model for them to just hire teachers through this pipeline.

As the Rural Residency Program got ready to welcome its second cohort in the fall of 2022, he was especially proud to share, "We didn't even have to advertise, and our second cohort is already full of residents that are all coming from these four rural districts." When asked why this model was preferable to the more traditional student teaching model, he replied:

> I think the biggest benefit to that is when you grow up in a certain community and you want to give back to your community, you come into your teaching position within that district with so much more knowledge about where your kids are coming from. Not to mention you are able to connect with students on a cultural level but also on a community level. It makes that experience automatically embedded into who you are as an educator versus going to a school district where you don't know anybody, you don't know the culture of the community and you are starting basically learning from scratch.

The residency model, which is gaining currency in teacher education programs across the country, stands in stark contrast to the traditional student teaching model, which has long been criticized as creating a gap between theory and practice. Without spending time in authentic K–12 classrooms, teacher candidates have no idea how the methods they are learning at the university work in front of real students, especially when those students come from culturally diverse backgrounds and have differentiated needs. So-called best practices are not always best for all students and are often much more difficult to implement when schools lack resources and teachers lack autonomy. There is also the issue of forgetting what you have learned when you don't put it into practice. As Jordon shared with us, "In our math classes . . . had we just learned it and not taught it, we probably would forget. When it's something hands-on, you don't forget." With university professors embedded at the school site, California State University, Fresno, professors can work closely with mentor teachers to make sure that candidates have ongoing opportunities to practice what they are learning in their courses and to reflect on their experiences in a timely manner.

In this chapter we explore the residency model more fully, drawing upon original research from two of the schools in our study that created residency programs for their candidates: California State University, Fresno's Rural Residency Program and New Mexico State University's BLOCKS Program. Before we delve into exactly what makes the residency model so powerful, however, it is important to understand why the traditional model of student teaching has persisted as it has, and why it is time for a change.

SO, WHAT'S WRONG WITH STUDENT TEACHING?

Traditionally, teacher preparation occurs in two very different educational contexts: Candidates work with college professors (from across the schools of education and liberal arts) on campus at the start of their programs to master academic content and methods. Then, in the final semester of their programs, they are moved to a local school site where they work alongside a classroom teacher to observe and practice their craft, which is commonly referred to as student teaching or clinical practice. In some respects, there are many good reasons for this design. Most teacher candidates have never taught before, and for many the last time they were even in a K–12 classroom was in high school. It is important that they have a firm grasp on the subject matter they are teaching, understand the socio-emotional development of the grade level that they are teaching, and know something about best practices in classroom management and student engagement before becoming fully certified teachers. University-based coursework covers these topics and gives candidates a chance to prove that they have mastered them through various assessments and assignments.

On the other hand, waiting until they have finished all their coursework before they spend quality time in K–12 classrooms makes it extremely difficult for candidates to know whether what they are learning in theory works in practice. Multiple studies have shown that it is common for teacher candidates to find that what they learned in their coursework is not feasible, applicable, on grade level, or aligned with school-based standards and assessments in the districts where they go on to student teach (Ball & Forzani, 2009; Forzani, 2014; McDonald et al., 2013; Meister & Melnick, 2003; Ronfeldt & Reininger, 2012).

Moreover, good teaching is comprised of much more than simply being able to convey content knowledge; teachers must understand the political and social contexts of schooling. As Moyer and Husman (2006) note, "Studies have led to a shared belief that teaching requires not only the ability to teach lessons, but also an understanding of the rules and routines of the school culture" (p. 38). When they start student teaching, for example, candidates may be confident in their mastery of the subject matter, but they are often unsure of how to navigate teaching content with issues such as lack of resources, high student absentee and dropout rates, and pressures to prepare students for high-stakes standardized tests. The misalignment between what they have learned in the university and what they experience in student teaching can lead candidates to feel frustrated, vulnerable, and unprepared, as well as dissuade some candidates from continuing to get their certification, thinking they just don't have what it takes to be an effective teacher (Ball & Forzani, 2009; Grossman et al., 2009; Zeichner, 2010).

The gap between theory and practice in traditional teacher education programs is further heightened in institutions where most faculty have never taught in K–12 settings themselves, have spent little to no time in the local schools where their candidates practice, and/or base their course content and curricula on generic ideas and materials about good teaching. Many teacher education faculty members still approach teaching as something scripted and regimented, relying solely on student memorization and standardized testing as signs of academic success. Likewise, university-based courses are often developed with the assumption that candidates will be teaching in classrooms that are primarily comprised of White, middle class, and English language dominant students. Thus, the materials they use and methods they promote are in danger of marginalizing or ignoring the experiences, assets, and needs of minoritized and low-income students. As Darling-Hammond (2006) suggests, teachers must be prepared to meet the unpredictable learning needs of all their students and become what she called "adaptive experts" (p. 305). This means that teachers need to know how to assess the competencies, prior knowledge, linguistic abilities, and assets and needs of diverse groups of students, and engage them in culturally relevant and differentiated instruction accordingly (Gay, 2002; Ladson-Billings, 2014; Paris, 2012).

Another issue is that the traditional design of teacher education programs, where university courses are frontloaded and classroom-based student teaching is tacked on to the end, suggests that what faculty members and classroom teachers contribute to the teacher education process are separate strands of knowledge. There is an implied hierarchy that faculty are the experts on educational theory, pedagogy, assessment, and academic achievement, while classroom teachers simply are there to model the process for candidates (Gorodetsky & Barak, 2008). This can make mentor teachers feel like they are simply supervisors rather than incredibly important co-educators in candidates' journeys to become teachers. As Zeichner (2010) suggests, "We also need to continue current efforts to involve cooperating teachers as full partners in our teacher education programs and stop treating them as second-class citizens who only provide places for our students to teach" (p. 53).

A related problem is that while classroom teachers likely appreciate the added support of a teacher candidate, they frequently have mixed feelings about ceding any level of control to a novice teacher, given that they are the ones ultimately responsible for the students in their class. If a candidate's lesson plan does not go well, mentor teachers must step in and redirect. Mentor teachers can also find the mentoring process to be added work that they don't have time for, get compensation for, or even receive recognition for (Zeichner, 2010). Significantly, in most underfunded and high-needs school districts, mentor teachers did their own training many years ago and have had few opportunities to engage in professional development. This can lead them to feel uncomfortable or even threatened when student teacher candidates try to introduce new pedagogical practices such as project-based learning and youth participatory action research, which they are unfamiliar with. In response to these kinds of critiques, many teacher educators have called for new models wherein faculty are more present and engaged in candidates' clinical experiences, working together with mentor teachers at an authentic school setting (Pang & Park, 2011).

Why Create Residencies?

There are many reasons why the residency model is preferable to student teaching. Candidates spend significantly more time in authentic classrooms. They are there 4 to 5 days, all day, all year round. Candidates get to be part of the entire school culture (including parent meetings and extracurricular activities); they are not just isolated in one classroom with one mentor teacher. Residencies attract local candidates who are committed to working in local schools. Many of the candidates went to the schools and have children in the schools where they are completing residencies. Residencies are more convenient for candidates who can't travel back and forth between school and their university, which in California State University, Fresno's case would be over an hour each way. Residencies also bridge the gap between theory and practice as candidates can try out what they are learning in content and methods classes, reflect, and redirect. Finally, by spending embedded time on school sites, faculty can confirm that what they are teaching candidates in methods courses is aligned with what is really happening in the schools (Gist et al., 2019).

Teacher Residencies and MSIs

While the residency model described at the beginning of this chapter is gaining traction in a variety of colleges across the country and has garnered the attention of the U.S. Department of Education's funding programs, it is particularly well aligned with the mission of MSIs. Our research underscores several reasons why MSIs are well positioned to successfully transition their teacher education programs to a residency model. For one thing, most MSIs have traditionally been community-engaged institutions that primarily draw their student bodies from local communities. As previously noted, many

MSI teacher candidates intentionally choose to get their degrees in the communities they grew up in and plan to teach in those communities upon getting their degrees. While part of this is that they have strong family ties in these communities, it is also indicative of their commitment to enrich underserved schools and dismantle barriers to educational equity that they themselves experienced. Many candidates don't even realize how much students appreciate representation in the classroom until they are in the front of the classroom themselves. Being able to do their clinical practice in their own communities not only makes the experience more meaningful and relevant for candidates, it can also be a source of immense pride.

Residencies are also a natural fit for MSIs because they are student-centered institutions where faculty value and support the development of the whole student, not just their academic scores. MSIs seek to provide wrap-around services that remove barriers for underserved students. Many MSI teacher education programs, for example, recognize that many low-income candidates simply cannot afford to spend an unpaid semester doing full-time student teaching. Other candidates do not have easy access to transportation or childcare, preventing them from going back and forth between the university and the schools in which the candidate teaches. The residency model removes many of these barriers.

It is also important to note that faculty at MSIs may be more willing to leave their offices and teach in nontraditional settings. Faculty at research intensive PWIs are rarely rewarded (and sometimes penalized) for community-based service work because it takes them away from research and publishing. By contrast, faculty at MSIs are explicitly hired because they are committed to working in the surrounding community. As one professor in our study shared:

> When I started at Fresno, during the interview they were very clear that the expectation for our faculty is to teach out at school sites, is to partner with districts, and to engage in that fieldwork. And if you're not willing to do that, then this is not the place for you. There's a very clear expectation from the leadership that we partner with schools in this way. So, if you want to teach this cohort of teacher candidates, then you need to go out to the school, period.

Like their students, many MSI faculty also have strong roots in the local community and look forward to opportunities to engage more deeply with their families, friends, and neighbors.

For the residency model to be successful, however, it is important to emphasize that it is not simply a matter of candidates spending more time in schools, or of faculty teaching their same courses but at a K–12 school site. It would be possible, for example, for candidates to work in classrooms in the morning and take courses in the afternoon at the same school site, and still never connect the two experiences. Major structural changes in program design require readdressing aligned issues of authority, time, power, and perspective among all cooperating stakeholder groups (Zeichner, 2010). A primary component of residencies is that professors, mentor teachers, and teacher candidates have a shared mission and common space to co-examine the core assumptions that guide their work together. These relationships must be built on mutual trust and collaborative teaching and learning (Darling-Hammond, 2006; Hollins, 2011). The research on residencies and university–school partnerships in teacher education has identified several core practices that need to take place for these models to be effective, sustainable, and ultimately transformative, including the following: (1) Faculty, mentor teachers, and candidates must have opportunities for co-teaching and co-learning, with the understanding that everyone has something valuable to contribute. Faculty cannot be the only experts. (2) While candidates go into classrooms much earlier than in traditional student teaching, there must be a structured model of gradual release, which helps scaffold the teaching process, giving candidates time to build confidence and develop a teacher disposition. (3) There needs to be sufficient administrative support that faculty and mentor teachers are not overloaded with paperwork and scheduling (Guha et al., 2016; Klein et al., 2013; Zeichner, 2010).

"WE WERE THERE FROM THE BEGINNING": CALIFORNIA STATE UNIVERSITY, FRESNO'S RURAL RESIDENCY PROGRAM

In California State University, Fresno's Rural Residency Program, faculty in residence stay with the same group of candidates for several semesters at the school site. The program coordinator notes that this is an important part of the program's cohesiveness and consistency, adding that "It almost feels like a homeroom experience" for candidates. The deputy superintendent at the Fresno County Superintendent of Schools agrees, describing the benefits of the residency model as such:

> The residency model just provides so many safety nets for teacher candidates to be mentored, to have access to resources, and to have direct access to professional development. What the residency model also does is it provides a professor in residence that is working hand in hand with the partnering district. The professor in residence is overseeing not only the teacher candidates and meeting their individual needs and requests, but they work with the mentor teachers. You get two individuals—your mentor teacher and your professor in residence.

He then contrasts this experience to student teaching, where:

> You are on your own. There is no one from the institution that is your classmate, that is working at the same school. You might be off on an island by

yourself. And it's just doing your coursework, doing your final student teaching really with minimal connection to the university itself. You are taking your classes and then you are going full-time student teaching and there is no cohesiveness to a theme or a platform so to speak of a model of pedagogy.

In addition to the daily interaction with and support of other teacher candidates and professors in their program, residents are intentionally matched with classroom teachers who are both exceptional in their craft and are fully on-board with the mentoring process. According to the faculty program coordinator, "Our team was intentional about the recruitment of mentor teachers. We didn't want it to be based on district seniority or anything of that nature, but really mentor teachers that the administrators had identified as having very strong pedagogical skills in the classroom." Mentor teachers, faculty in residence, and candidates all engage in mutual professional development to better understand what co-teaching and co-learning looks like. The faculty program coordinator also shares that:

> What I appreciate most about teaching this course is the collaborative nature of sharing ideas and experiences that challenge us most as educators. We all work together to improve our teaching and effectiveness in the classroom. The [way] residents engage in this continuous improvement has always been rewarding. Their curiosity, vulnerability, and willingness to engage in best practices is inspiring. The course also allows me to learn alongside teacher residents. We all improve our practices through this important work.

Candidates in California State University, Fresno's Rural Residency Program also have dedicated coaches, who are typically retired teachers, who are compensated through the program to provide candidates with additional support and ensure that there are no problems or miscommunications between candidates and their mentor teachers. As previously noted, this can make a critical difference in the success of the residency model, because generally faculty and mentor teachers are already at their capacity. Moreover, because coaches generally have years of teaching experience themselves, they serve as an additional source of knowledge and professional mentorship for the residents.

Another prominent feature of California State University, Fresno's Rural Residency Program is that it is built on a concept of gradual release, wherein mentor teachers scaffold the teaching process and slowly let candidates take on greater responsibility in the classroom. For example, at the beginning of the school year candidates help with classroom setup, learn classroom procedures, and introduce themselves to school support staff. As the school year goes on, candidates are required to communicate with at least two families with positive feedback about their child, regularly observe other classrooms in the school, engage in curriculum development, begin co-teaching, and teach one or two content areas a day by themselves. By the end of the year, they are teaching by themselves at least 2 days a week in addition to helping to set up and run parent–teacher conferences and extracurricular activities. In the last semester they also do what's called a 4-week takeover and are further qualified to be substitute teachers when needed. The gradual release schedule is chronicled in the program's weekly newsletter, which includes detailed instructions for mentor teachers, coaches, and candidates so that everyone is on the same page. When asked about the impact of this model, one resident explained:

> It has been a great experience. We started when the teachers were just getting their classrooms set up. Even before students stepped on campus, we were already there working with our mentor teachers. That was amazing to see every step of becoming a teacher. The first couple of weeks we just observed, but little by little with our mentor teacher's help they would have us do little lessons here and there. We gradually started taking over. First it was specific lessons, then it was a couple of hours a day and then half a day. By next month we will be taking over the class for the whole day. Now we know our students. We know their learning abilities and their styles. We really get that whole feeling of being a teacher in the classroom. It kind of feels like we are the teacher in the classroom since we were there from the beginning.

Another candidate noted similarly, "It really helps me to feel like I'm coming into my own. Being able to take the information I'm learning and then apply it has been a big help to me."

Throughout this process, faculty in residence, coaches, and mentor teachers work actively together to observe and provide feedback on candidates' lesson plans, classroom management skills, interactions with students, levels of professionalism, and communication with parents. In addition to providing candidates with constructive and detailed feedback, candidates have regular opportunities to reflect on their practice and engage in peer observation. As the program coordinator notes of this experience:

> We also ask them to do observations in each other's classrooms and in each other's schools. So, take the day to go over and look at another context. I find them very invested in the outcomes of the school and very invested in the success of the schools in the community. So, it's very empowering for them. They definitely care about one another. They advocate for one another.

Candidates in the California State University, Fresno, Rural Residency Program are also required to select a focal student with whom they develop a close relationship throughout the entire school year. Candidates learn about their student's cultural backgrounds, assets, and interests, allowing them to develop personalized assessments and lesson plans for them, and tracking their progress over time. One candidate describes the impact of this approach:

> I think it really showed us that when you take the time to work with students one-on-one to learn about them and learn what they need from you, you are going to be able to see that progress. For me personally, I know that we developed a really close relationship because of the time we spent working together and because I took the time to ask her 'What do you like learning about? What types of books do you read at home? Who takes care of you after school and what kind of activities do you do?' That emphasized to me the importance of getting to know your students in order to tailor their education to them.

A focus on student care and healthy development is also one of the themes of the Rural Residency Program in the Kerman School District. Commonly referred to as trauma informed practice (Thomas et al., 2019), candidates are encouraged to develop holistic support systems that lift students up rather than push them out of school. According to the district superintendent:

> Candidates will do the residency and then they'll go into their first year of teaching with a myriad of tools and strategies revolving around trauma informed practices. They are learning how to deal with some of the impacts of trauma. It allows our residents the opportunity to go through a professional development series addressing questions such as: What are some of the things that you can look for as a teacher to better meet the needs of your children? What are the methods of mindfulness and verbal de-escalation strategies that a teacher may need going into their first year of teaching that they may never have had the opportunity to learn? One example is being able to see the signs of early intervention and prevention for students who may be experiencing trauma or adverse childhood experiences. Maybe there are different strategies and skills sets that teachers need to deescalate crises in the classroom. [They are] gaining experience into ways to assist kids on how to regulate their behavior.

As suggested in the beginning of this chapter, candidates in the residency program are particularly invested in the health and well-being of their students, because they themselves experienced many of the same traumas growing up. Candidates are accurately aware of what it feels like to live in poverty or to be English language learners and are more likely to recognize the signs and need for intervention, as well as to approach students from an asset-based perspective rather than dwelling only on their challenges. Teacher candidates Adriana and Jordon, who we introduced at the beginning of this chapter, will likely be hired in the Kerman School District upon completing the program. As one professor at California State University, Fresno State observed, by the time that residents completed the program and were hired by the district, "They had gone through a year of the school's or the district's professional learning. So, they knew all the initiatives. They knew all the curricula. They felt like they were part of the community. They knew all the teachers onsite." The program coordinator likewise shared with us:

> With the residency programs it's really nice because we have such a strong relationship with the district. We walk in with the understanding that the teacher candidates are sort of being groomed for their school sites, embedded within their school community, being a part of the community. The district is chomping at the bit to give them offers already. The Deputy Superintendent at the Office of Education is an advocate for each and every single one of them. He told them all, "I will help you find a classroom upon graduation.'"

From the deputy superintendent's perspective, hiring the candidates who go through the Rural Residency Program is a no-brainer: "Being in that residency model where you are giving back to your own community, you are already walking into that experience with so much more passion about the community where you grew up."

"THEIR TIME IN THE CLASSROOM IS JUST AS IMPORTANT AS MINE": NEW MEXICO STATE UNIVERSITY'S BLOCKS PROGRAM

Another residency model that we identified in our research was the BLOCKS Program, which was created at New Mexico State University (NMSU) in 2001. As part of BLOCKS, NMSU partners with elementary schools in neighborhood school districts where, like California State University, Fresno's Rural Residency Program, teacher candidates spend four mornings a week working in school classrooms, after which they attend seminars taught at the same school site by NMSU faculty. Through their participation in BLOCKS, teacher candidates have early, increased, and progressively responsible experiences in authentic classroom settings, including lesson planning, student assessment, co-teaching, parent conferences, and supervising extracurricular activities. Activities and assignments from the seminars are thus fully integrated within the students' fieldwork. In just 2 semesters, students log over 360 hours of contact with children, teachers, staff, and the classroom and school culture before they transition to their full-day student teaching. As one candidate shared:

> We're here at 7:30 in the morning when school starts and we're with the students until they go to lunch. It is very helpful to see what your day is going to be like when you do become a teacher and have your own classroom. You see the stresses of every day. You see the lesson plans, what goes into the classroom environment, behaviors, you see everything that is involved in the classroom. It

just brings more hands-on learning. I enjoy it because it has opened my eyes to what real life is going to be like after college.

Like California State University, Fresno's Rural Residency Program, BLOCKS classroom teachers are careful to make sure that candidates are comfortable and are eased into increased levels of responsibility. As one classroom teacher explained, "I've always found that I like to approach things the way I would want someone to expose me to something that is new, and so I ease them in, and I do what makes them feel comfortable. I'm always checking with them. If you're not comfortable, if you're not ready, we can wait a couple of days, another week. I do ease them into the semester. I want to make sure they're comfortable with it." Other classroom teachers emphasized the importance of modeling teaching practices for candidates while also giving them the flexibility to assert their own individuality. As one teacher told us, "I do a lot of modeling. To see how the classroom can run and just give them strategies to use in the classroom. I model everything for them. This is how I do it. Feel free to copy that. If you have your own way, that's great. You don't have to do it like I do." BLOCKS candidates appear to have internalized the need to find their own teacher identity and to approach students in ways that feel authentic. As one candidate shared with us:

> One thing I really enjoyed about my experience is it showed me how to be a flexible teacher, because obviously you have one plan in mind, and sometimes the students have another plan. So, you have to learn how to accommodate how the students are feeling, what is going on, and you have to be able to change out what your original plan was. It shows you how to be flexible, how to go with the flow and how to keep an organized yet fun classroom, so that students can be successful and learn.

Also, like California State University, Fresno, BLOCKS is a nonhierarchical model based on mutual respect and full collaboration wherein professors and classroom teachers are both viewed as having equally valuable knowledge about teaching and learning. While their individual roles may be different, the common thread is the belief that everybody involved in BLOCKS is in some way a teacher, and further that everybody can learn from one another. The fact that some BLOCKS faculty members were once public school teachers themselves—in the same elementary schools no less—certainly creates a foundation on which to build trust and mutual respect. Both parties share ownership of the design, content, and success of the program. In this sense, the BLOCKS program seeks to break down traditional hierarchies between professors, teacher candidates, and classroom teachers.

One example of this co-ownership is found in the way that BLOCKS professors take the time to learn about the larger contexts in which local schools operate and try to align their course content and methods courses accordingly. One faculty member told us that open communication is key, sharing that they meet with cooperating teachers at the beginning of every semester to share their syllabus and assignments, and directly ask for their suggestions for improvements. This same process repeats at the end of the semester to provide for mutual reflection on best practices. Another professor shared similarly: "At the beginning of the semester we meet with all the practicum [mentor] teachers, give them a copy of our syllabus and expectations, ask them for any questions they have."

The BLOCKS program faculty co-director noted that other faculty members at NMSU are, in fact, constantly engaging in professional development with the teachers in the BLOCKS schools, underscoring the importance of mutual learning and continuous conversation and dialogue between classroom teachers and professors. When speaking of an upcoming professional development workshop, she shared that the BLOCKS co-director "has been very clear that it is not going to be one way, that faculty is not going to do these workshops. It is going to be circular and we're going to learn from those classroom teachers as well." As a result of these workshops, faculty and classroom teachers are more likely to send consistent messages to candidates. One BLOCKS faculty member, for example, told us that at the beginning of the school year she hadn't realized that the school curriculum had changed, and she was instructing her candidates to teach material that was no longer considered grade-level appropriate. Through her participation in BLOCKS and her close relationship with classroom teachers, she was able to confirm that her coursework was sending candidates' mixed messages and was able to revise her course with the appropriate modifications.

Like California State University, Fresno's Rural Residency Program, which uses retired teachers as coaches, NMSU graduate assistants have successfully adopted roles as daily liaisons between NMSU professors and the teachers and administrators at the local school sites. As one classroom teacher described the BLOCKS graduate student facilitator at her school: "She comes every single day. She monitors them [candidates] daily and she walks in every day just to make sure things are going smoothly. Sometimes it is a five-minute walk-in thing. Sometimes she is there for an hour. She's the one that is the day-to-day person. Any concerns, anything, we address through her." Again, this removes a lot of the stress that faculty and mentor teachers might experience in terms of scheduling meetings, making announcements, and distributing important documents. It also provides candidates with an additional layer of support. According to one graduate assistant, "We really need to always be in communication. We have their cell phone numbers, so I can reach them anytime. The students can come to us anytime. I've had [candidates] text me at all hours of the night and in the morning."

Both faculty and mentor teachers agree that through the BLOCKS model, candidates are quicker to develop teacher dispositions and identities. According to one faculty member:

> It's not like they are progressing towards being a teacher, they feel themselves as teachers. They have that confidence. They have that motivation. They have that attitude within themselves. They are sure they belong. They know that they want to do that. It is a perception, but also through words, through conversations, through interactions, body language sometimes.

BLOCKS candidates are also able to raise real—rather than hypothetical—problems of practice in their coursework, enabling them to both identify, pilot, and assess alternative teaching strategies concurrently. When asked what she thought were some of the strengths of the NMSU teacher education program, one professor referred to the program's focus on application:

> When I see them [the candidates] in the classroom and I see them integrating practices that we've done in the courses, then it's one of those "they're using it and it's working" type of moments. You see that they are practicing what they are learning in theory. They're applying it as well.

Another professor agreed, noting that there is a big difference between assigning a textbook or case study and having candidates try out different pedagogical approaches with real students. She noted that "I can have them read about it and have them do case studies all day long, but until they must manage children.... you can't really get that experience."

In the traditional student teaching model, candidates do not spend a significant amount of time outside of their individual classroom placement. This can end up providing them with a narrow or even distorted understanding of the politics of teaching. By contrast, in BLOCKS, professors and mentor teachers make a concerted effort to teach the candidates as much as they can about the politics of the school district and even of the state department of education. According to one professor, "I know in my experience, when I was doing BLOCKS, we would always leave 20 to 30 minutes to talk about, okay, what is going on in the classroom? What is going on in the district?" In this respect, BLOCKS gives candidates a clear sense of the obstacles they will face. This means helping candidates adjust to some of the less ideal aspects of teaching—in this case having to do with a lack of resources and high pressure to teach to the test. While professors and classroom teachers do not mean to discourage candidates, facing certain realities of teaching gives candidates a "heads-up," which can prevent praxis shock and burnout down the road.

Another teacher disposition that BLOCKS candidates learn is the importance of adopting a growth mindset with all students. BLOCKS classroom teachers model these dispositions for candidates by giving candidates leeway to experiment, providing them with actionable and asset-based feedback, and allowing them opportunities to self-reflect. As one candidate described her experience with her mentor teacher in BLOCKS,

> When I would teach, she would sit back, let me do my thing, figure out my mistakes and she would just watch me. And afterwards she would not only critique me and tell me 'Okay, but this is also how you could do better.' But she also would compliment me on what she thought I did right. Which was really nice to see both sides of the spectrum and be complimented as well as to see what I could improve on.

When the time is right, BLOCKS teachers are more than ready to step aside for candidates, as one teacher told us: "I always make them feel like they are the priority, because when it comes time for that, I always say I need to step down for you. I will step down for you because we are here to help you. So, when you're ready, you just need to tell me and whatever I'm doing can wait. I can do it later, or I can do it before, or I can do it the next day. I make them feel like their time in the classroom is just as important as mine."

Residency programs like NMSU's BLOCKS and California State University, Fresno's Rural Teacher Residency Program highlight how MSIs build upon the promise of institutions' investment in their local communities. Analogous to the way that the flipped classroom has transformed pedagogical practices within college classrooms, these residency models outline the value added of flipped structures that support and build upon students' deep investment in learning within their future teaching environments. Thus, rather than reinscribing asymmetrical power relationships between universities and community partners, these models are emblematic of institutional commitments to stronger place-based partnerships that embody the promise of shared leadership between university teacher education programs and the rich knowledge emergent from daily problems of practice from experienced district educators. As evidenced by the beneficiaries and participants of these programs, implementing these approaches to teacher preparation requires a culture of reciprocity and respect, and a willingness to innovate beyond traditional bureaucratic structures. At the heart of participants' reflections, we find how their willingness to engage in alternative approaches to teacher preparation is consistently animated by the belief that these approaches are truly in the service of all members of the community—from the youth at the schools and their families to teacher candidates themselves.

CHAPTER 6

Where Wisdom Sits
Teacher Preparation and Community Engagement

As is common among MSIs in general, we found many examples of ways in which their teacher education programs used community-based activities as a way of helping candidates to broaden their perspectives, to recognize assets and opportunities in communities that they were unfamiliar with, and to learn directly from community members about their cultural traditions, history, and values. In the case of Stone Child College (SCC), having elders from the reservation serve as educators, historians, and preservers of knowledge and culture was a natural part of Indigenous culture. According to SCC's then president, a core component of the college is, in fact, to provide a community service: "What makes us unique is that we provide culturally relevant education that embodies our tribal cultural values, our history, our language, and of course the contemporary issues we face." This is not typical, however, of the way most cultures view the relationship between the school and the surrounding community. As NMSU professors Prentice Baptise and Jeanette Haynes-Writer (2009) suggest, "Too often a school and its staff constitute an island, which is physically within, but culturally and epistemologically removed, from the surrounding community" (n.p.).

In this chapter we look at a range of ways that community engagement can be incorporated into teacher education, including having candidates make regular home visits and volunteering for a broad array of community-service activities. We found multiple examples of teacher candidates volunteering at community sites and events, such as library book drives, health fairs, homeless shelters, and food banks. In some cases, the goal was to help parents and families become more involved in their children's education by feeling more connected to the schools and teachers that cared for their children, or to help parents become more aware of the range of services that schools and districts had to offer them. In other cases, the goal was more oriented toward community empowerment, as candidates provided families with direct support such as providing glasses for kids, or helping to donate and distribute food, clothing, financial aid, or medical services to families in need.

Still other examples of community engagement in the schools we visited included field trips to historical and cultural sites; organizing parent and adult education programs such as learning to use new technologies or English language learning; mentoring high school students (especially those interested in a career in teaching); and facilitating cultural activities such as literature clubs in inner city apartment complexes or organizing music and crafts festivals where parents, children, and educators could all share a common uplifting experience.

Finally, all the programs we visited had some component of inquiry, also referred to as teacher research, action research, and participatory action research. In these cases, candidates took the initiative to systematically ask questions and collect data about a particular problem or issue and work with other educators and community members to provide solutions. For example, a candidate might research the impact of student hunger on learning, and as a result help organize a school community garden or food drive. Another example might be a candidate researching student racial profiling or bullying, leading to the creation of community-wide awareness campaign or of free workshops. In the remainder of this chapter, we look at some of these activities in greater detail from the various perspectives of faculty, teachers and school administrators, candidates, and families.

HOME VISITS

Commonly, the only reason why teachers reach out to parents beyond regularly scheduled teacher–parent conferences is because a child is struggling academically, has gotten into trouble at school, has a high absentee rate, or is being bullied by other students (Garcia & Guerra, 2004). Put another way, it's rare for teachers to reach out to families for a positive reason, simply to let them know that their child is doing well, or to inquire about how they might better support students and their families. By contrast, the teacher candidates at the MSIs we visited were encouraged to make calls and visits to students' families simply to let them know that their child is working hard and making progress. When parents hear positive things about their children, they are more likely to trust the teachers and the schools when they need assistance, recognizing that the schools are invested in their children and in their families (Epstein, 1995; Henderson & Mapp 2002). This is especially the case for parents whose own experiences in school were negative or troublesome and who have no positive experiences with teachers to reflect on.

California State University, Fresno's California Mini Corps (CMC) tutors, for example, are required to make at least three regular home visits to parents of the children they tutor. As CMC faculty co-director explains, "That is one of the requirements of the program because we feel it's very important that they're making that connection with families, that they are see where these kids live, and just to know more about the child." One CMC tutor shared that "Home visits was one of my favorite things to do. We would go into their homes, and we would introduce ourselves to the parents, let them know who we are in the classroom, and inform them about the resources at the school and how we could help."

It is important to understand that while CMC tutors themselves come from migrant backgrounds, that does not necessarily mean that they know about the circumstances of an individual child's home life. One CMC faculty member shared an example from her own experience: "I remember this one child, and their house was made of aluminum siding. That broke my heart. Even though we may be poor, we have certain essentials. And sometimes to find out their living conditions, it is very important." A CMC student tutor similarly shared:

> I remember that one of the schools I worked with asked for volunteers to go and give lessons at these really small houses in the fields. And we took food with us, and I mean, yes, my parents were low-income, but I think I was exposed to new experiences because I went there, and I got to see that people were living in these houses that were ready to fall [apart]. . . . After they had this really good meal, they all sat down and participated and talked, and we told them about these different resources that we offered. And they talked about how sometimes they didn't have enough money to pay for some bills or even have enough food, or they've got to stretch it out. And I think when students have those things going on at home and then come to school, they are going to be more worried about what is going on at home. . . . You don't know what is going on at home that is going to stop them from learning.

When CMC tutors make these visits, they are required to fill out a form on which they check off the items that they discussed with parents. According to the CMC co-director, "It could be just explaining the program, how they are getting extra support. It could be sharing strategies that probably can help their child." She adds that she is acutely aware that migrant families want a better life for their children but often don't know anything other than life in the fields and are unfamiliar with the range of financial and counseling services that could help their children attend college, concluding that "It's about knowledge." Yet as CMCI tutors reminded us, it was also about demonstrating love and care for their children, and those small acts of generosity went a long way toward helping parents be more trusting of their students' teachers. One CMC tutor shared the importance of something as simple as bringing vegetables to share a salad:

> We brought vegetables to make like a salad, and we brought fruit, and we brought juice. And they were so excited. All the kids gathered around. The parents didn't know how to thank us for it. That feeling just melted my heart

away. And then after they had this really good meal, a very healthy meal, they all sat down and participated and talked, and we told them about these different things that they, the resources that are offered. And they were very surprised that they had all this help.

It is important to underscore, however, that the goodwill generated by these home visits was not unidirectional. According to one CMC member:

> Sometimes the parents would feed us. We would go visit our students, and they'd feed us. They would share, and that's one thing that we've learned that our migrant students and our migrant community, even though they have a little, they share everything. They're very giving, and that's how we've been taught since we were young. Even if it's one cookie, you split it up between everybody. That way everyone has something to eat. And as soon as we got there, they would try to offer us whatever they had, which I thought was amazing.

COMMUNITY SERVICE

In addition to regular home visits, teacher candidates for the CMC Program at California State University, Fresno volunteer a minimum of 6 hours per semester to do community service activities. Sometimes these are directly related to what is going on at the school. For example, CMC students often stayed late to tutor migrant students during parent–teacher conferences or to provide translation for families who did not speak English. CMC tutors also volunteered at a broad range of community sites such as the Visalia Rescue Mission, VOTA Campaign, the Community and School Beautification Project, the Bulldog Pantry, and the Arne Nixon Paint-a-Mural Program. Finally, the CMC Program also engaged candidates as helpers, facilitators, and presenters in more ambitious projects such as a FAFSA project, wherein eight different local colleges engaged CMC tutors to help families complete financial aid forms; an annual Migrant Parent Conference; a California State University, Fresno Teacher Fair; or a Chicano Latino Youth Conference. As with the home visits, CMC students are required to fill out a form reflecting on these experiences, which explicitly asks CMC tutors to "Explain your involvement and how you and the community benefited from this service."

The men in Jackson State University's (JSU) Call Me MISTER (CMM) program are also expected to support local communities through internships and service activities. In fact, the concept of "servant leadership" or leadership as an act of service is at the core of the CMM program. According to the CMM program director:

> Community engagement was always a central part of the JSU Call Me MISTER program. Some of the volunteer and internship activities were very traditional

such as assisting in elementary and middle school extra-curricular and after school programs, while others varied greatly. Misters participated in a wide variety of activities such as facilitating literature clubs in inner city apartment complexes, conducting conflict resolution trainings for Pre-K–12 students through the Goldring/Woldenberg Institute of Southern Life, facilitating HIV prevention workshops for incoming freshman at JSU, interning at the Mississippi Broadcasting Early Childhood division where they hosted educational events and conducted reading sessions, and serving as counselors and facilitators in a Texas community college STEM program.

He further explains that the MISTERs have a voice in determining which program and community activities they are most interested in, sharing:

> I think that community engagement is one portion of teacher education that we don't emphasize enough. Focusing on skills and strategies is necessary, but it's caring that really drives the profession. Providing students with opportunities to utilize what they are learning in their teacher education program in community settings often enables them to see the impact that they are making (or the potential to make as teachers) quicker. They are more likely to be shown appreciation by students and parents and are more often able to really recognize the impact that they make in children's lives since their focus isn't purely on academic performance.

PARENTAL EDUCATION

We also found multiple examples of ways that the teacher education programs facilitated parent education programs, recognizing that the more information and skills parents had, the more supportive they could be of their children. Many of these events are centered on English language learning and financial security. One of the most prominent programs we encountered was called *Tech at Home*. Developed and organized by a New Mexico State University (NMSU) faculty member, this program engaged parents in the La Cruces and surrounding public schools in 15 hours of technology instruction. Working alongside their teacher candidates and their children, parents were given an iPad or Chromebook and learned how to use the Internet to find resources, such as the school website, and how to contact the principal and teachers. The program was offered in Spanish given that it was the primary language spoken. As part of the program, parents were directed to write an email to the principal or teachers as a way of learning how to better communicate. At the end of the program, parents were given the computer they worked on to keep. According to the program director:

> We've been doing it with fourth, fifth and six grade student parents. It creates a lot of goodwill to the point where the parents want more, because we are

delivering it in their language, and we are teaching them. Whoever needs extra help, we help them. What we were doing was getting the preservice teachers to go out with the instructors and be helpers. The candidate's role was to assist the parents. My goal was that I wanted them to have experiences working with parents. To not be distant from parents. . . . The idea was to get into a more positive process where the parents are learning, the children are there and then they can interact.

A teacher candidate who participated in the *Tech Goes Home* program confirmed that the program had the intended effect of helping parents feel more engaged with their children's education and helping teacher candidates have more positive experiences with parents:

> Once I did my first *Tech Goes Home* program, I fell in love with the program, especially with involvement of parents, how engaged they got, how motivated they were to learn and to be part of something that will help their kids in the long term with their education. We began by teaching parents technology, helping them set up the IPADs and teaching them how to navigate technology. We told them they could go to McDonalds, which has free WIFI that they can connect with. And they use this not only to navigate their kids' schools, but also to pay their bills. The program was in Spanish. You would see the kids teaching the parents, different things that they had to learn together. . . . *Tech Goes Home* helps parents to be aware that there are teachers that are really wanting to make them part of the school environment and they don't have to feel left out and that they can reach out to us when they really have a question, or they need something. That we are there to help them, not just to teach their kids but to involve them in our classrooms.

FIELD TRIPS

Several of the programs we visited organized field trips specifically designed to help candidates experience a new cultural perspective. Stone Child College (SCC) teacher candidates, for example, joined candidates from another Tribal College, Salish Kootenai College, for a 2-day field trip to the Montana School for the Deaf and Blind (MSDB). MSDB, which was about 90 minutes away by car, "provided an opportunity for candidates to observe multiple teachers providing instruction to a diverse student population, not just culturally, but also in terms of learning exceptionalities." According to the SCC candidate handbook:

> [Teacher candidates] prepare lessons to present to the children at the school about the seven Indian Tribes in Montana, adding not only to their understanding

about the great diversity among the American Indians in Montana, but also giving the children at the MSDB some insights about the great diversity among tribal cultures, traditions, and languages within the Tribes located in Montana. During a tour of the school, students will have the opportunity to see many teachers using multiple methods of providing instruction to a multitude of children with exceptional learning needs. The experience is intense and thought-provoking as students self-check their attitudes and reflect on the varying needs of children.

Another example of taking candidates on the road was at California State University, Fresno, where faculty organized an overnight trip to Los Angeles for candidates to visit the Museum of Tolerance. The trip was free, as the museum was offering grants for groups of teachers and was tailoring the experience specifically to meet the needs and interests of the group they hosted. Funding included a charter bus and driver, hotel accommodation for one night, and 2 days of programming at the museum, including lunch both days. The museum also gave teacher candidates free resource guides on service learning. For many of the teacher candidates, it was the first time they ever left home or stayed at a hotel.

As part of planning the trip to the Museum of Tolerance, California State University, Fresno teacher education faculty members along with CMC faculty co-directors asked the teacher candidates to identify a speaker. The candidates chose Sylvia Mendez, who was at the center of a major court case on school desegregation for Latinx students in 1946. According to the faculty organizers:

> We requested her as a speaker for lots of different reasons. Her story is a critical part of history, education, and social justice in the U.S. The *Mendez v. Westminster* case, which ended de jure segregation in California, paved the way for *Brown v. Board of Education* and subsequent integration and civil rights work. I don't think her family was migrant, but they were farmers and immigrants from Mexico so many of our students could see themselves and their families in her story.

One faculty member further emphasized how important it was for students to know about historical events that had a huge impact on their own communities but may not have reached the history books, sharing that:

> I do believe this was the first-time students heard a firsthand story of a historical event outside of their own families. It connected them to the past, to history, to a personal equity journey in the context of being Mexican or Latinx in California, farm workers, immigrants, so many intersectionalities. We felt it was important for the candidates to see themselves represented in the history of California, as shapers of society, as agentive change makers—to awaken them

to possibilities that had been intentionally hidden from them—to engage them as teachers for social justice and equity. To see how the case helped shape their current experiences in the school system and that we still have so much more to do.

When candidates visited the part of the museum that focused specifically on the Holocaust, they were able to make connections among different histories of injustice. After the visit to the museum, candidates engaged in reflective inquiry, including creating posters around questions such as, "How can I relate curriculum to the lives of my students?" and "How can I give students the opportunity to take charge of their own educational endeavors?"

INQUIRY, ACTION RESEARCH, AND ADVOCACY

Another common theme we found among the teacher preparation programs we researched was the inclusion of inquiry or action research projects leading to the creation of collaborative solutions to school and community-based inequities. While the focus and scope of these research projects looked different at each of the four schools, in all cases the project prompted candidates to better understand the root causes of educational inequities and find ways to be advocates for students and their families. The projects also encouraged candidates to engage in what Cochran-Smith and Lytle (2009) have coined "inquiry as stance," suggesting that asking critical questions about issues of equity and challenging the sociopolitical contexts of education is something that teachers should adopt as a habit of mind, not as an extra activity.

For example, NMSU's teacher education program includes a thematic unit on Funds of Knowledge (Gonzalez et al., 2005) in which candidates must choose a focal student, visit their home, and interview family members. Afterwards, candidates write a three- to five-page report on what they learned, including "Knowledge of the child and the family and their cultural practices, resources, and histories." Finally, working in pairs, candidates create an "integrated curriculum unit consisting of five individual lessons based on this new knowledge." Candidates were instructed that:

> The unit must be integrative and cross-disciplinary and should indicate which subjects per New Mexico Standards and Benchmarks will be covered. . . . Each of the lessons must be fully informed by a critical perspective analysis engaging students in identifying examples of social injustice, inequity, discrimination, violation of human rights and dignity, and other forms of dehumanization and oppression.

As part of this critical analysis, at least one of the lesson plans needed to "provide an opportunity for students to take action in their community," shifting it from a straight lecture to a form of youth participatory action research (YPAR). YPAR showed up in another course at NMSU, which focused specifically on adult and family literacy. Candidates were required to conduct a literature review on research around literacy learning and the politics of teaching literacy in schools, looking at "both deficit and transformative practices." Candidates then developed their own research questions and engaged in original research with local families. Rather than traditional interviews with parents, candidates planned joint family engagement activities, such as "a drawing or writing workshop, or a read aloud with a discussion." Candidates were further directed, "You might focus on the family's reading and writing experiences as young children, adolescents, as adults, and what their dreams are for their own children. You might have them contrast their experiences in school with their children's experiences with school." Significantly, the professor of this course emphasized the importance of mutual respect, underscoring that "This requires getting to know families to establish trust and to feel safe in your classroom. Some families did not have good experiences in their own schooling." After completing the family activities, candidates were asked to reflect on questions such as:

> What did you find? What did you expect? What knowledge did parents go away with and what evidence do you have for this? What insights and comments did parents give? Most importantly, what knowledge did you come away with?

As candidates reflected on these questions, they developed new literacy teaching units, and at the end of the semester, they wrote an advocacy plan for policymakers and administrators to improve literacy learning and disrupt inequitable and discriminatory practices.

While research and inquiry are in themselves worthwhile, advocacy remains an important and sometimes overlooked piece of the puzzle. At California State University, Fresno, for example, teacher candidates in the Rural Residency Program are required to lead collaborative inquiry projects with students in their elementary school science classes. In this respect, candidates are asked to engage elementary students as key stakeholders, working together to transform the classroom through research and project-based learning. According to an article coauthored by the California State University, Fresno, faculty member who designed and taught the class, Christina Macias, many candidates were surprised to learn of the socioeconomic barriers that prevented many students from connecting with science education. For example, two candidates noted that their students demonstrated a wealth of knowledge about projects such as Legos, iPhone, and computer games and yet "While 10 out of 15 students interviewed had some concept of technology, most had limited access to such devices that were reserved as behavior rewards, provided for academically advanced students, or limited to children with the means to own such tools outside the school" (Macias et al., 2021, p. 9).

When asked to reflect on why this was a problem, the teacher candidates noted that "If a student cannot connect to what is being taught, they are most likely going to check out of the lesson early on. However, if we can engage them by talking about something that they already know about or something that excites them, they will want to participate and continue learning," a revelation which prompted the candidates to "forgo a more traditional method of teaching science concepts and instead found ways to transform student learning experiences by utilizing the resources students were drawn to, thus ensuring science learning for those traditionally denied access" (Macias et al., 2021, p. 12). Over time, the candidates began to view their students "not only as leaders, but as agents of community change," as reflected in the range of advocacy projects students helped to create, such as bringing a mobile food truck to campus to address lack of healthy snacks, bringing a chicken coop to campus so students could observe live pets in their science learning activities, or creating solar powered chargers for students to charge their computers. According to Macis et al. (2021):

> Collaborative inquiry contributed to nuanced and thoughtful solutions to student identified problems, most particularly access to such learning experiences as highlighted in nearly all of the projects. From science curricular access to proper nutrition, the elementary school students decided which science tools and resources facilitated solutions to barriers in their own classrooms and communities. Such efforts were possible through collaboration with their Pre-Service Teachers (PTs) who engaged in teaching and learning *alongside* their students. (p. 18)

Macias et al. concluded that "It is rare for PTs to have opportunities to learn about and advocate for their learners in this way. The data driven collaborative inquiry process enables PTs to speak with confidence (and evidence) to teachers and administrators" (p. 11).

Of note, California State University, Fresno tries to integrate some form of candidate inquiry into every course and clinical experience. They even created a series of courses called Inquiry and Puzzles or Practice (IPOP) 1, 2, and 3. According to our interview with the faculty members who were responsible for creating these courses:

> We asked faculty what they thought we needed more of in our program, and they all said inquiry. And we envisioned an inquiry course that spans the entire length of the teacher education program, that works alongside of the other courses so that the students are learning how to engage in inquiry processes and then applying those inquiry processes to puzzles of practice as they moved into teaching disciplinary literacy and content areas. . . . We just felt we needed

more time than a single course because inquiry isn't course bound. We wanted to emphasize the process, not the product because inquiry is the foundation of good teaching. Without inquiry, you never get better. We wanted to instill a habit of inquiry in the candidates before they got out of the program so that when they got into their classrooms as teachers of record that they just thought inquiry was what teachers do.

Another important reason why candidates are asked to engage in original research and inquiry is to prepare them for graduate school and other leadership positions in education. At JSU, for example, the members of Call Me MISTER (CMM) were required to engage in research projects "as soon as they hit campus." One research topic, for example, asked candidates to do original interviews with African American male elementary school teachers about student achievement in their classrooms. After completing the research, candidates learned to analyze and write up their findings and are given opportunities to present their findings at conferences and other educational forums. As one professor at JSU explained, the impact of this exercise is not only to give candidates research, writing, and critical thinking skills, but to help them be competitive should they decide to go to graduate school. Candidates are encouraged to share their research at conferences, which gives them much needed confidence when talking to their peers and other professionals. According to the CMM program director:

> The main thing is that I want them to get the experience and see what it's like being involved in research, but also helping to build their confidence and let them know that, look, not only can you talk and work with young children, but you can do the same thing with your peers and with other professionals. Again, we want them to be able to stand up and speak for what they believe pretty much around anyone. . . . Again, we want them to not just go into the classroom to be qualified teachers, but we want them to be able to be leaders in their community.

Teacher candidates at JSU were quick to confirm that the research process did indeed make them feel like they were leaders. As one candidate told us, "Usually in high school you just pull something off the internet and do it. We had to go out to the different schools and talk to the different teachers and interview them. Sit down and interview them and see how the kids reacted to them. I felt like I was doing research instead of using somebody else's research. I feel like I was doing something important." While many colleges and universities try to steer away from any hint of engaging in politics, JSU wants its teacher candidates to go into the classroom with "lots of tools to be able to draw on" and further acknowledges that some of its graduates might well go into administration of public policy. The CMM program director believed that by engaging candidates in research, public speaking, and advocacy, "whichever route they choose to take they will be equipped to handle it."

The CMM program provides each cohort with a mini grant that supports travel to different conferences where they can present their research findings. The program director believed that "They've been well received at the conference, and they've done a good job. Again, the main thing is that I want to them get the experience and see what it's like to be involved in research and helping to build their confidence. Let them know that not only can you talk and work with young children, but you can do the same things with your peers and with professionals. We want them to be able to stand up and speak for what they believe in."

The range of community-focused programming highlighted across all four MSIs underscores how teacher candidates preparing within these institutional contexts are primed to recognize their role as educators as embedded actors within their local communities. Beyond their preparation to effectively deliver instructional content, these opportunities underscore the purposeful efforts to model relational humility between teacher candidates, youth, families, and the broader communities within their respective districts. Importantly, all these programs reveal that communal engagement is far from a casual add-on to teacher candidates' formation; on the contrary, these opportunities are a cornerstone upon which candidates deepen their commitments to their communities while also engaging in meaningful introspection of the ways in which they approach these relationships. These opportunities to engage in scaffolded and guided reflection alongside their peers, instructors, and mentors offers the necessary space for candidates to articulate, clarify, and challenge how they connect their role as educators within a broader effort to contribute to their local communities.

CHAPTER 7

A Call to Action

There is much to learn from Minority Serving Institutions, and the first step is to acknowledge the range of promising practices that the field of teacher education can adopt and modify to their respective contexts. Indeed, we have an opportunity to turn to MSIs as leaders in the field of teacher education given their long-term commitment to educating a diverse nation (Conrad & Gasman, 2015). To make substantive changes in teacher education, to create richer and more supportive experiences for teacher candidates of color, and to ensure that all students, especially students of color, benefit from the pedagogy of teachers of color, we must act. We offer recommendations in the following areas:

DIVERSIFY THE TEACHING PROFESSION

We must diversify the teaching profession both for demographic parity and because teachers of color serve as important mentors, role models, and advocates for students and communities of color. At the same time, while the presence of same-race teachers has some merit, it is not a panacea. Teachers come with intersectional identities, including differences based on gender, race, class, ethnicity, language, and so on. These identities do not always translate into being able to understand the experiences of all students of the same race.

INTEGRATE CULTURALLY RELEVANT PEDAGOGY

Candidates need much more than one or two multicultural education courses, as there is great variation both across and within racial and ethnic groups. Asian Americans, for example, are seen as a "model minority," but this does not hold true when disaggregating the Asian American pan-ethnic marker to acknowledge the histories of forced migration and displacement that disproportionally affect recent waves of Southeast Asian immigrants' material conditions in the United States. Likewise, an African American teacher may know a lot about racism against African Americans and engage in coalitional learning opportunities to address colorism across racial groups yet may have limited access to the relevant embodied knowledge on the effects of Indigenous dispossession and linguistic policing mediating Latinx and Native American youths' experiences in educational settings.

To adequately prepare all teachers to work with students of color, we thus need to integrate issues of culture and equity across all of teacher education coursework and practice. It cannot be seen as an add-on or specialty, or solely the responsibility of only teachers of color. This comprehensive approach also means that both content courses and methods courses need to address culturally relevant teaching. Moreover, it is important that teacher candidates have consistent opportunities to reflect on their own education and cultural experiences as a gateway to cultivating an empathic, caring, humble, and culturally proactive teaching, and to model this same process for future students.

EXPAND STUDENT TEACHING AND CLINICAL PRACTICE

Teacher education must fill the gap between coursework and clinical practice, resequencing the traditional model of first doing coursework on campus and then doing practice later in school-based settings. Universities and schools need to develop partnerships and residencies where candidates begin working in schools from the outset of their teacher education preparation. These university–school partnerships also cannot be dictated totally by the university; they must strive to be mutually beneficial by explicitly accounting for the power differentials between collaborators and focusing on co-teaching and learning. Of note, having designated coaches or graduate students dedicated to supporting teacher candidates in their school placements can supplement the labor undertaken by faculty and mentor teachers by having a designated point person that can maintain open channels of communication.

Learning to teach under the support of a mentor teacher should be modeled and scaffolded, allowing candidates to gradually increase their responsibility in the classroom from observation to co-teaching to solo teaching. Importantly, our suggestions for integrating teacher candidates within the school community must include opportunities for candidates to engage beyond curriculum development and teaching. Fostering opportunities where candidates contribute to the broader efforts to support a culture of belonging within the school is equally critical for their development, including opportunities to design the classroom learning environment; facilitate student assessment, assemblies, and school trips; conducting parent–teacher conferences; and embedding themselves within the extracurricular activities of the school.

RECRUIT FORMER K-12 TEACHERS TO THE FACULTY

More teacher education faculty members need to (1) build upon prior professional experiences as K–12 educators; (2) be representative and responsive to diverse cultures and experiences; (3) stay up to date as school policy and mandates change to properly support candidates' development; and (4) be open to co-teaching and learning from working teachers. Faculty must be accessible and available to candidates, modeling an ethos of care, high support, and high expectations. Institutional support for faculty is critical to ensure these attributes are acknowledged and rewarded for working with students and out in the community. This approach requires institutional leaders to recognize the multifaceted labor of preparing future educators and accounts for the various aspects that all too often remain hidden or are merely considered an add-on to their effectiveness as instructors.

PROMOTE COHORT MODELS

Candidates do better in cohort models or communities of practice. On the one hand, cohorts serve as a "safety net" for candidates that feel isolated, and on the other hand, cohorts keep candidates accountable. As evidenced by two of the programs in the MSIs in this study, there are multiple ways of cultivating these communities of support for teacher candidates. The models from these MSIs underscore the promise and value of groups focused on shared identities, such as students of migrant experiences in California to Black men educators in Mississippi. In creating these cohort models around a common identity, we underscore the importance of engaging in asset-driven approaches that not only inoculate candidates from damaging racial tropes of unbelonging, but also transform the candidates' commitment to the educational calling with a sense of expansive possibility and solidarity.

PROVIDE WRAPAROUND CANDIDATE SUPPORT

Prerequisites to becoming a good teacher should not depend solely on GPAs and test scores; teaching is about much more than content knowledge. The exemplary approaches from the MSIs in this project show the critical value of supporting candidates with additional instructional support and tutoring. Yet, in framing the provision of these services, teacher education programs must not fall into the trappings of push-out narratives that undermine candidates' capacity to hone their emerging talents. What is clear from prospective candidates in our study is that the barriers they face in their preparation as teachers span beyond academic demands. For candidates who come from first-generation and low-income backgrounds, for example, programs must also account for the financial aid, time when courses are scheduled, transportation, Internet accessibility, and access to supplemental stipends for administrative fees—from childcare to testing fees. Recognizing these structural barriers is necessary for programs that strive to ensure proactive responsiveness for teacher candidates' entire well-being.

FOSTER COMMUNITY ENGAGEMENT

It is also important that candidates spend quality time working in the communities where their students live. This time can be in the form of living within the communities where they teach, engaging in consistent service activities responsive to their communities' immediate needs, deliberately participating in home visits, offering free or affordable educational opportunities for parents and families, or engaging in participatory action research to better understand community cultures and needs. In the same way that we urge programs to approach supporting teacher candidates through wraparound services, nurturing a culture of communal engagement further integrates an ethos of committed solidarity. At the same time, we also underscore how these forms of community engagement must be designed with the appropriate critical reflection for candidates to consistently interrogate their own biases and assumptions lest we replicate harmful surface-level stereotypes.

RESPECT THE TEACHING PROFESSION

Some of the teachers who inspire and support their learners are individuals who have overcome adversity in their own education and want to pave the way for educational equity for future generations. We caution engaging in the mere symbolic appreciation of educators' resilience and commitment to the profession. On the contrary, educators are charged with the critically significant role of nourishing the consciousness of future generations. Equitable pay, public investment in educators' continuing professional development, and transparency in opportunities for teachers' advancement are a handful of concrete practices that ensure our appreciation for educators is not solely a matter of rhetorical affirmations but also enacted through the deliberate allocation of resources and compensation.

COMMUNICATE MESSAGES OF SUCCESS

One of the hallmarks of MSIs is the communication of success to students in both the curriculum and the co-curricular context of the institution. Students tend to be greeted with messages of "you belong" and "you can succeed" from the moment they step on campus. Among the MSIs featured in this book, students spoke candidly of the benefits afforded by participating in programs where instructors assumed students' future success and fully believed in the assets that students brought to the classroom. Teacher education candidates had no reason to doubt their worth or their ability to make contributions to students in the classroom.

CONSIDER THE IMPORTANCE OF LOVE

As we have shown, nurturing a love of teaching, teachers' love of students, and students' love of teachers are essential components of teacher education at MSIs. Yes, content is important, as we have demonstrated—especially content that is responsive to learners' varied experiences and identities—but love and care are foundational to good teaching, effective learning, and the longevity of teachers of color in the teaching profession. As Bettina Love (2019) has previously stated, "I do not think white teachers enter the profession wanting to harm children of color, but they will hurt a child whose culture is viewed as an afterthought" (p. 18). Thus, to cultivate an approach to teacher education rooted in love is to engage in purposeful acts that invite students' multiple selves into their learning experiences. As Love further argues, "the question is not: do you love all children? The question is: will you fight for justice for Black and Brown children? And how will you fight? I argue that you must fight with the creativity, imagination, urgency, boldness, ingenuity, and rebellious spirit of abolitionists to advocate for an education system where all Black and Brown children are thriving." From MSIs, we can learn the promising practices that can teach us what a love for teaching looks like when racial equity is front and center in the way we prepare future generations of educators.

Final Thoughts

Since the conclusion of our research project, we have witnessed increased volatility on the political landscape for public education in the United States. Educators face the pressures of state legislatures skeptical of the suitability and value of culturally responsive teaching. Invoking misleading understandings of critical race theory, dozens of state representatives have sought to curtail the prominence of racially aware curricula among K–12 and postsecondary education alike.

Alongside these efforts to constrain students' intellectual and psychological well-being, federal and state legislatures have continued an anemic resolve in their responses to mitigate the relentlessness of gun violence in school settings. Merely halfway through 2022, we have already endured over two dozen shootings on school grounds in the United States, resulting in 83 injuries or deaths of youth and educators (*Education Week*, 2022). And, as evidenced by the descriptions of the programmatic structures of the various models used at these four MSIs, we engaged in our data collection alongside our colleagues at these MSIs prior to COVID-19's disruptive impact on both instructional approaches and our communal well-being.

These changes have invariably shifted the future of teacher education programs in ways that are not fully captured through our participants' reflections. Yet we find that any hopeful vision for teacher education in the face of a politically precarious future, the prospect of ongoing violence at schools, and the enduring effects of COVID-19 require us to learn and engage with bold and innovative leadership that can imagine otherwise. Through their unwavering commitment to place-based programming and solidarity, to integrating students' identities as an essential component of effective pedagogy, and to respect teacher candidates' ongoing introspection and self-examination, these MSIs offer models of how teacher education programs can adapt to meet the current challenges of educational equity in the United States.

APPENDIX A

The Study

Our book is the result of a 3-year, mixed method research project funded by the W.K. Kellogg Foundation. Our goal for this research was to identify innovative and successful models within MSI teacher education programs that would further the goal of diversifying the teaching profession, increase academic achievement for students of color, and close opportunity gaps for underserved students including low-income, first-generation, immigrant, and bilingual students. We sought to identify four MSIs with demonstrated leadership potential in the field of teacher education and preparation. We disseminated a call for proposals to all MSIs with teacher education programs in their academic offerings. We invited institutions to submit an application that highlighted their successful curricular offerings for teacher preparation, as well as proposed areas of innovation to improve the ways in which they were preparing their students to become more effective teachers.

We selected one institution from each major MSI sector—HBCUs, TCUs, HSIs, and AANAPISIs—from the applicant pool. Each of the selected MSIs received a capacity-building grant to implement initiatives that they proposed—initiatives designed to innovate their teacher education programs. We spent time on each of the four MSI campuses, learning about their successful practices in teacher education.

INSTITUTION AND PROGRAM DESCRIPTIONS

New Mexico State University is recognized as a Hispanic-serving institution and serves over 29,000 students. The College of Education offers undergraduate and graduate degrees in early childhood education, elementary and secondary education, counseling and educational psychology, special education, and educational leadership, among other specialties. New Mexico State provides access to two Hispanic-serving school districts in the Las Cruces region—serving over 38,000 low-income and English language learner students—where prospective teachers work as they prepare for careers in education. In 2001, the university created BLOCKS, an innovative new model for university–school partnerships and student teaching. University-level courses are taught on-site at local elementary schools, where student teachers, certified classroom teachers (supervising teachers), and faculty work collaboratively to design curricula, test new pedagogy, assess student performance, and create teaching portfolios. Students enrolled in the BLOCKS program spend four mornings a week working in classrooms, after which they attend seminars taught in the school by New Mexico State faculty. Activities and assignments from the seminars are thus fully integrated within the students' fieldwork. In just 2 semesters, students log over 360 hours of contact with children, teachers, staff, and the classroom and school culture before they transition to their full-day student teaching.

Jackson State University, an HBCU, strives to create and promote practices that assist students of color in the successful completion of teacher education programs. In 2012, Jackson State partnered with Clemson University and the W.K. Kellogg Foundation to establish a Call Me MISTER program in the deep South. Call Me MISTER students receive tuition assistance, professional development opportunities, testing workshops, and academic and social mentoring provided by a program coordinator and faculty coach. In exchange, these students commit to teaching for one year in Mississippi public schools for each year that they receive financial assistance.

Stone Child College (SCC) is a 2-year TCU located in a rural part of north-central Montana. The college is geographically situated in the center for the Rocky Boy Indian Reservation, one of the smallest reservations in Montana. Chartered by the Tribal government in 1984, SCC primarily serves the Chippewa Cree tribe, whose membership is about 7,000 people. Approximately 4,000 of its members live on the reservation. SCC is governed by a Board of Directors that includes Tribal Council members, members of the community at large, and representatives from two local school districts (the Box Elder School District and the Rocky Boy School District). Most SCC students are recruited from these two school districts, and SCC's governance committee also includes at least one student representative. Like many Tribal colleges, the community surrounding SCC is economically depressed, with an average of 60–75% unemployment throughout the year. Over 95% of SCC students are Pell Grant eligible. The average student requires some remedial coursework, particularly in the STEM areas. The college accepts students who have not received a high school education, many of whom enter with a GED. The average age of students used to be over 30 years old, but in recent years it has dropped to closer to 23 years old. The college provides students with financial aid, transportation, childcare, and other basic needs that support their retention and success.

With a student body that is 60.4% Latino and 10.8% Asian, California State University, Fresno (HSI and AANAPISI) serves a diverse community that is both urban and rural. Over 200,000 immigrants live in the Fresno County region, comprising 22% of the population. The Kremen School of Education and Human Development at California State University, Fresno, thus has an ongoing commitment to the development of future bilingual–bicultural certified teachers. The university offers its teacher education students opportunities to get their teaching degrees in conjunction with the California State Mini Corps program.

Founded in 1967 in collaboration with California's Department of Migrant Education, this statewide program is committed to the success of migrant students, particularly those who do not speak English or are bilingual. The California State University, Fresno Mini Corps program pairs former migrant students, now studying to be teachers, with current migrant students for one-on-one tutoring, mentoring, and home visits. In 2015, California State University, Fresno Mini-Corps students collaborated with 165 teachers in local school districts, providing direct instruction to 676 pupils—all of whom were either Hispanic or Asian American/Pacific Islander. At the university, Mini Corps students participate in a cohort model with additional supervision, including support with teacher certification exams, portfolio development, and career counseling.

OUR APPROACH

To gather documents and recruit participants, we used stratified purposeful sampling (Patton, 2002). Participants represented various stakeholder positions within teacher education. While we learned about the teacher education programs from internal documents, the principal method of data gathering was semi-structured interviews. Of note, we recruited students who were persisting and moving ahead and faculty and staff who were contributing to building and implementing the teacher education initiatives. Across the institutions, we interviewed 80 students, faculty, and staff affiliated with the focal programs. Through this process, we were able to gather broadly comparable data across stakeholder positions (Bogdan & Biklen, 1998) and, at the same time, to create spaces in which participants could share their individual experiences and interpretations of their perspectives. In each interview, follow-up questions focused on opportunities for participation across stakeholder groups that contributed to student persistence and learning. We viewed our interviews as conversations and presented ourselves as fully engaged participants in a conversation while encouraging participants to do most of the talking. We met with participants on campus in private settings and in locations that were familiar to them. We began by asking open-ended questions to explore and document participants' stories of success in teacher education. Each interview lasted 30 to 60 minutes (Glesne & Peshkin, 1992). We developed lines of questioning to encourage study participants to recall experiences and information (Kvale, 1996; Yin, 2012). We frequently invited participants to make sense of a story or observation or to connect a story or observation with a comment and phrase that had come up earlier in the interview.

To analyze the data, we conducted open coding (Creswell, 2012) focused on practices that contributed to persistence, success, and learning in teacher education. Open coding enables researchers to examine the direction in which to take research, allowing the researchers to be more selective and focused conceptually on the issue being studied (Glaser, 2016). We each used in vivo codes (Charmaz, 2011) to highlight participants' interpretation of educational opportunity as well as process codes (Bogdan & Biklen, 2007) to identify activities that they recognized as empowering students to persist and acquire knowledge. We identified, compared, and refined multiple codes through two additional rounds of review and deliberation. Redundant codes were collapsed to generate larger categories that spoke to our research questions, which lead to the development of major themes.

Throughout the study, we took various measures to ensure the validity of the findings. First, as researchers, we engaged in frequent conversation in the field during and after the interviews to tease out potential biases (Conrad et al., 1993). We also developed memos in the field and added them to our database. Second, every member of the team spent a substantial amount of time reviewing and evaluating the data to determine coding categories and themes, thereby ensuring inter-rater reliability or the degree of agreement among the participants (Yin, 2012). Third, as we analyzed transcripts, we held regular meetings to share and deliberate on codes we had developed individually. In these meetings, we tested one another's codes and emerging themes against transcripts and one another's interpretations and perspectives. Finally, we collected institutional documents from several sources and used these to triangulate data obtained through our interviews, comparing interview data with them.

POSITIONALITY

No study is disconnected from the experiences, dispositions, and perspectives of its researchers; the current study is no different. In designing this study, we were continuously aware of our position as three researchers (two women, one man, one person of color, and two bilingual scholars) from PWIs. From this perspective, we approached this study with the belief that MSIs are leaders. Their effective practices in improving student success in teacher education (as documented in this study) are indicative of their knowledge of the communities—their values, histories, and traditions—they serve (Yosso, 2005). This approach is reflected in the ways we shaped the collection of data, conducted the analysis, and discussed the data. To mitigate the influence of our positionality, we had regular conversations as a research team as to how our race, gender, language, and status shaped our data collection and data interpretation. We challenged each other and learned from each other as we conducted the research and wrote this book.

Notes

Introduction

1. MSIs include Historically Black Colleges and Universities, Hispanic Serving Institutions, Tribal Colleges and Universities, Asian American and Native American Pacific Islander Serving Institutions, Predominantly Black Institutions, Native American Non-Tribal Serving Institutions, Alaska Native Serving Institutions, and Native Hawaiian Serving Institutions.

Chapter 1

1. Carver-Thomas found that "three in four teachers of color work in the quartile of schools that serve the most students of color" (2018, p. 14).

Chapter 4

1. Familiar name in Spanish

References

Achinstein, B., Ogawa, R. T., Sexton, D., & Freitas, C. (2010). Retaining teachers of color: A pressing problem and a potential strategy for "hard-to-staff" schools. *Review of Educational Research, 80*(1), 71–107.

Assaf, L. C., Garza, R., & Battle, J. (2010). Multicultural teacher education: Examining the perceptions, practices, and coherence in one teacher preparation program. *Teacher Education Quarterly, 37*(2), 115–135.

Aronson, B., & Laughter, J. (2016). The theory and practice of culturally relevant education: A synthesis of research across content areas. *Review of Educational Research, 86*(1), 163–206.

Bain, R. B., & Moje, E. B. (2012). Mapping the teacher education terrain for novices. *Phi Delta Kappan, 93*(5), 62–65.

Ball, A. F., & Tyson, C. A. (2011). *Studying diversity in teacher education*. Rowman and Littlefield.

Ball, D. L., & Forzani, F. M. (2009). The work of teaching and the challenge for teacher education. *Journal of Teacher Education, 60*(5), 497–511.

Blake, D. (2018). Motivations and paths to becoming faculty at Minority Serving Institutions. *Education Sciences, 8*(1), 1–16.

Bogdan, R., & Biklen, S. (1998). *Qualitative research for education*. Allyn & Bacon.

Bogdan, R. C., & Biklen, S. K. (2007). *Qualitative research for education: An introduction to theory and methods* (5th ed.). Allyn & Bacon.

Brayboy, B., & Castagno, A. E. (2009). Self-determination through self-education: Culturally responsive schooling for Indigenous students in the USA. *Teaching Education, 20*(1), 31–53.

Bullough, R. Jr., Clark, C., Wentworth, N., & Hansen, J. (2001). Student cohorts, school rhythms and teacher education. *Teacher Education Quarterly, 28*(2), 97–110.

Canrinus E., Klette, K., & Hammerness, K. (2019). Diversity in coherence: Strengths and opportunities of three programs. *Journal of Teacher Education, 70*(3), 192–205.

Carter Andrews, D., Richmond, G., & Marciano, J. J. (2021). The teacher support imperative: Teacher education and the pedagogy of connection. *Journal of Teacher Education, 72*(3), 267–270.

Carver-Thomas, D. (2018). *Diversifying the teaching professions through high retention pathways*. Learning Policy Institute.

Castro Samayoa, A., & Gasman, M. (2019). *A primer on Minority Serving Institutions*. Routledge Press.

Center for American Progress. (2017). *America needs more teachers of color and a more selective teaching profession.* https://www.americanprogress.org/article/america-needs-teachers-color-selective-teaching-profession/

Chapman, T. K. (2011). *History of multicultural education: Teachers and teacher education.* Routledge Press.

Charmaz, K. (2011). Grounded theory methods in social justice research. In N. K. Denizen & Y. Lincoln (Eds.), *The Sage Handbook of Qualitative Research* (4th ed., pp. 359–380). Sage.

Cochran-Smith, M., & Lytle, S. (2009). *Inquiry as stance: Practitioner research for the next generation.* Teachers College Press.

Conrad, C., & Gasman, M. (2015). *Educating a diverse nation: Lessons from Minority-Serving Institutions.* Harvard University Press.

Conrad, C., Haworth, J. G., & Millar, S. B. (1993). *A silent success.* The Johns Hopkins University Press.

Creswell, J. W. (2012). *Educational research: Planning, conducting, and evaluating quantitative and qualitative research.* Pearson Education.

Cross, B. (2005). New racism, reformed teacher education, and the same ole' oppression. *Educational Studies: Journal of the American Educational Studies Association, 38*(3), 263–274.

Darling-Hammond, L. (1998). *Unequal opportunity: Race and education.* Brookings Institution. https://www.brookings.edu/articles/unequal-opportunity-race-and-education

Darling-Hammond, L. (2006). *Powerful teacher education: Lessons from exemplary programs.* Jossey-Bass.

De Brey, C., Snyder, T. D., Zhang, A., & Dillow, S. A. (2021). *Digest of education statistics 2019 (NCES 2021-009).* National Center for Education Statistics, Institute of Education Sciences, U.S. Department of Education.

Dilworth, M. E. (1992). *Diversity in Teacher Education: New Expectations.* Jossey-Bass.

Dilworth, M. E. (2012). Historically Black Colleges and Universities in teacher education reform. *Journal of Negro Education, 81*(2), 121–135.

Dinsmore, J., & Wenger, K. (2006). Relationships in preservice teacher preparation: From cohorts to communities. *Teacher Education Quarterly, 33*(1), 57–74.

Dixon, D., & Griffin, A. (2019). *If you listen, we will stay.* The Educational Trust.

Duncheon, J. (2021). Making sense of college readiness in a low performing urban high school: Perspectives of high achieving first generation youth. *Urban Education, 56*(8), 1360–1387.

Education Week. (2022, October 31). School shootings this year: How many and where. https://www.edweek.org/leadership/school-shootings-this-year-how-many-and-where/2022/01

Edwards, C. (2019). Overcoming imposter syndrome and stereotype threat: Reconceptualizing the definition of a scholar. *Taboo: The Journal of Culture and Education, 18*(1), 18–34.

Epstein, J. L. (1995). School–family–community partnerships: Caring for the children we share. *Phi Delta Kappan, 76,* 701–712.

Forzani, F. (2014). Understanding "core practices" and "practice-based" teacher education: Learning from the past. *Journal of Teacher Education, 65*(4), 357–368.

References

Galman, S., Pica-Smith, C., & Rosenberger, C. (2010). Aggressive and tender navigations: Teacher educators confront Whiteness in their practice. *Journal of Teacher Education. 61*(3), 225–236.

Garcia, G. (2019). *Becoming Hispanic Serving Institutions: Opportunities for colleges and universities*. Johns Hopkins University Press.

Garcia, S., & Guerra, P. (2004). Deconstructing deficit thinking: Working with educators to create more equitable learning environments. *Education and Urban Society, 36*(2), 150–168.

Gasman, M. (2007). *Envisioning Black colleges: A history of the United Negro College Fund*. Johns Hopkins University Press.

Gasman, M., Castro Samayoa, A., & Ginsberg, A. (2017). *A rich source for teachers of color and learning: Minority Serving Institutions*. Penn Center for Minority Serving Institutions.

Gasman, M., & Conrad, C. (2013). *Educating all students: Minority Serving Institutions*. Penn Center for Minority Serving Institutions.

Gasman, M., & Esters, L. (forthcoming). *The power of Historically Black Colleges and Universities*. Johns Hopkins University Press.

Gasman, M. B., Baez, B., & Turner, C. (2008). *Understanding Minority-Serving Institutions*. SUNY Press.

Gasman, M. B., & Nguyen, T. H. (2019). *Making Black scientists*. Harvard University Press.

Gay, G. (2002). Preparing for culturally responsive teaching. *Journal of Teacher Education, 53*(2), 106–116.

Gay, G. (2010). *Culturally responsive teaching: Theory, research, and practice*. Teachers College Press.

Gist, C. (2016). Voices of aspiring teachers of color: Unraveling the double bind in teacher education. *Journal of Family Issues, 52*(8), 1026–1053.

Gist, C., Bianco, M., & Lynn, M. (2019). Examining grow your own programs across the teacher development continuum: Mining research on teachers of color and nontraditional educator pipelines, *Journal of Teacher Education, 70*(1), 13–25.

Glaser, B. G. (2016). Open coding descriptions. *Grounded Theory Review: An International Journal, 15*(1). http://groundedtheoryreview.com/2016/12/19/open-coding-descriptions

Glesne, C., & Peshkin, A. (1992). *Becoming qualitative researchers: An introduction*. Longman.

Gonzalez, N. E., Moll, L., & Amanti, C. (Eds.). (2005). *Funds of knowledge: Theorizing practices in households, communities, and classrooms*. Lawrence Erlbaum Associates.

Goodwin, A. L. (1997). Historical and contemporary perspectives on multicultural teacher education: Past lessons, new directions. In J. King, E. Hollins, & W. Hayman (Eds.). *Preparing teachers for cultural diversity*. Teachers College Press, 5–22.

Goodwin, A. L. (2004). Exploring the perspectives of teacher educators of color: What do they bring to teacher education? *Issues in Teacher Education, 13*(2), 7–24.

Gordon, J. (2000). *The color of teaching*. Routledge Press.

Gorodetsky, M., & Barak, J. (2008). The educational-cultural edge: A participative learning environment for co-emergence of personal and institutional growth. *Teaching and Teacher Education, 24*(7), 1907–1918.

Gorski, P., & Parekh, G. (2020). Supporting critical multicultural teacher educators: Transformative teaching, social justice education, and perceptions of institutional support. *Intercultural Education, 31*(3), 265–285.

Grant, C., and Gibson, M. (2009). Diversity and teacher education: A historical perspective on research and policy. In A. F. Ball & C. A. Tyson (Eds.), *Studying diversity in teacher education*. Rowman and Littlefield.

Grossman, P., Hammerness, K., & McDonald, M. (2009). Redefining teaching, re-imagining teacher education. *Teachers and Teaching: Theory and Practice, 15*(2), 273–289.

Guha, R., Hyler, M., & Darling-Hammond, L. (2016). *The teacher residency: An innovative model for preparing teachers*. Learning Policy Institute.

Hartlep, N. (2013). *The model minority stereotype: Demystifying Asian American success*. Information Age Publishing.

Haynes-Writer, J. (2008). Unmasking, exposing, and confronting: Critical race theory, tribal critical race theory and multicultural education. *International Journal of Multicultural Education, 10*(2), 1–15.

Haynes-Writer, J., & Baptiste, H. (2009). Realizing students' everyday realities: Community analysis as a model for social justice. *Journal of Praxis in Multicultural Education, 4*(1), n.p.

Henderson, A., & Mapp, K. L. (2002). The impact of school, family and community connections on student achievement. National Center for Family and Community Connections in Schools. Retrieved at: ED474521.pdf

Hollins, E. (2011). Teacher preparation for quality teaching. *Journal of Teacher Education, 62*(4), 395–407.

Hollins, E. (2015). *Rethinking field experiences in preservice teacher preparation: Meeting new challenges for accountability*. Routledge Press.

Hollins, E., & Crockett, M. (2012). *Briefing paper for the CAEP commission on clinical standards*. http://caepnet.org/~/media/Files/caep/accreditation-resources/clinical-experiences-preparation.pdf

Holmes Group. (1995). *Tomorrow's schools of education: A report of the Holmes Group*.

Howard, T. (2001). Powerful pedagogy for African American students: A case of four teachers. *Urban Education, 36*(2), 179–202.

Hsieh, B., & Nguyen, H. T. (2020). Coalitional resistance: Challenging racialized and gender oppression in teacher education. *Journal of Teacher Education, 72*(3), 355–367.

Ingersoll, R. (2001). Teacher turnover and teacher shortages: An organizational analysis. *American Educational Research Journal, 38*(3), 499–534.

Jackson, T., & Kohli, R. (2016). Guest editors' introduction: The state of teachers of color. *Equity and Excellence in Education, 49*(1), 1–8.

Jones, R. A., Holton, W., & Joseph, M. (Winter, 2019). Call Me Mister: A Black male grow your own program. *Teacher Education Quarterly*, 55–68.

King, J. (1991). Dysconscious racism: Ideology, identity, and the miseducation of teachers. *Journal of Negro Education, 60*(2), 133–46.

King, J., Hollins, E., & Hayman, W. (1997). *Preparing teachers for cultural diversity*. Teachers College Press.

Klein, E. J., Taylor, M., Onore, C., Strom, K., & Abrams, L. (2013). Finding a third space in teacher education: Creating an urban teacher residency. *Teaching Education, 24*(1), 27–57.

References

Koenig, R. (2021). *The college program: Attracting—and retaining—male teachers.* Ed Surge. https://www.edsurge.com/news/2021-07-21-the-college-program-attracting-and-retaining-black-male-teachers

Kohli, R. (2018). Behind school doors: The impact of hostile racial climates on urban teachers of color. *Urban Education, 53*(3), 307–333.

Kozol, J. (2012). *Savage inequalities: Children in American schools.* Crown Press.

Kvale, S. (1996). *Interviews: An introduction to qualitative research writing.* Sage Publications.

Ladson-Billings, G. (1995). Towards a theory of culturally relevant pedagogy. *American Educational Research Journal, 32*(3), 465–491.

Ladson-Billings, G. (2005). Is the team all right? Diversity and teacher education. *Journal of Teacher Education, 56*(3), 229–234.

Ladson-Billings, G. (2014). Culturally relevant pedagogy 2.0: A.K.A. the remix. *Harvard Educational Review, 84*(1), 74–84.

Lansing, D. R. (2014). Preparing teachers to contribute to educational change in Native communities: Navigating safety zones in praxis. *Journal of American Indian Education, 53*(3), 25–41.

Lee, T. (2011). Teaching Native youth, teaching about Native peoples: Shifting the paradigm to socioculturally responsive education. In J. E. King, E. R. Hollins, & W. C. Hayman (Eds.), *Preparing Teachers for Cultural Diversity* (pp. 275–294). Teachers College Press.

Lopez, J. (2017). Factors influencing American Indian and Alaska Native postsecondary persistence: AI/AN millennium falcon persistence model. *Research in Higher Education, 59*, 792–811.

Love, B. (2019). Dear white teachers: You don't love Black and Brown children in ways that matter. *Education Week, 38*(26), 18.

Macias, C., Shin, M., & Bennett, L. (2021). "They were teaching me!": Reimaging collaborative inquiry with elementary students in science teacher education. *Journal of Science Teacher Education, 33*(5), 1–22.

Marchitello, M., & Trinidad, J. (2019). *Preparing teachers for diverse schools: Lessons from Minority Serving Institutions.* Bellwether Education Partners.

McCarty, T., & Lee, T. (2014). Critical culturally sustaining: Revitalizing pedagogy and indigenous education sovereignty. *Harvard Educational Review, 84*(1), 101–124.

McDonald, M., Kazemi, E., & Kavanagh, S. (2013). Core practices and pedagogies of teacher education: A call for a common language and collective activity. *Journal of Teacher Education, 64*(5), 378–386.

Meister, D., & Melnick, S. (2003). National new teacher study: Beginning teachers' concerns, *Action in Teacher Education, 24*(4), 87–94.

Melnick, S., & Zeichner, K. M. (1995). *Teacher education for cultural diversity: Enhancing the capacity of teacher education institutions to address diversity issues.* National Center for Research and Teacher Learning, (pp. 1–27).

Melnick, S. L., & Zeichner, K. M. (1997). Enhancing the capacity of teacher education institutions to address diversity issues. In J. E. King, E. R. Hollins, & W. C. Hayman (Eds.), *Preparing teachers for cultural diversity* (pp. 23–29). Teachers College Press.

Milner, H. R. (2008). Critical race theory and interest convergence as analytic tools in teacher education politics and practices. *Journal of Teacher Education, 59*(4), 332–346.

Milner, H. R. (2010). What does teacher education have to do with teaching? Implications for diversity studies. *Journal of Teacher Education, 61*(1–2), 118–131.

Milner, H. R. (2012). But what is urban education? *Urban Education, 47*(3), 556–561.

Moll, L., Amanti, C., & Gonzalez, N. (1992). Funds of knowledge for teaching. *Theory Into Practice, 31*(2), 132–141.

Moyer, P., & Husman, J. (2006). Integrating coursework and field placements: The impact of preservice elementary mathematics teachers' connections to teaching. *Teacher Education Quarterly, 33*(1), 37–56.

National Center for Education Statistics. (2022). *Racial/ethnic enrollment in public schools*. U.S. Department of Education, Institute of Education Sciences. Retrieved from: https://nces.ed.gov/programs/coe/indicator/cge.

Nguyen, M. H. (2019). *Building capacity at Asian American and Native American Pacific Islander Serving Institutions (AANAPISI): Cultivating leaders and civic engagement through federal policy*. Ph.D. Dissertation, UCLA.

Noddings, N. (1992). *The challenge to care in schools*. Teachers College Press.

Nuñez, A. M., Ramalho, E., & Cuero, K. (2010) Pedagogy for equity: Teaching in a Hispanic-Serving Institution. *Innovation in Higher Education, 35*, 177–190.

Olson, B., & Buchanan, R. (2017). Everyone wants you to do everything: Investigating professional identity development of teacher educators. *Teacher Education Quarterly, 44*(1), 9–34.

Pang, V., Gresham, A., & Martuza, V. (1997). Removing the mask of academia: Institutions collaborating in the struggle for equity. In J. King, E. Hollins, & W. Hayman (Eds.), *Preparing teachers for cultural diversity* (pp. 53–70). Teachers College Press.

Pang, V., & Park, C. (2011). Creating interdisciplinary multicultural teacher education: Courageous leadership is crucial. In A. Ball & C. Tyson (Eds.), *Studying diversity in teacher education* (pp. 63–80). Rowman and Littlefield.

Paris, D. D. (2012). Culturally sustaining pedagogy: A needed change in stance, terminology, and practice. *Educational Researcher, 41*(3), 93–97.

Patton, K., & Parker, M. (2017). Teacher education communities of practice: More than a culture of collaboration. *Teaching and Teacher Education, 67*, 351–360.

Patton, M. (2002). *Qualitative research and evaluation methods*. Sage Publications.

Petchauer, E. (2018). *Navigating teacher licensure exams: Success and self-discovery on the high stakes path to the classroom*. Routledge Press.

Petchauer, E., & Mawhinney, L. (2017). *Teacher education across Minority-Serving Institutions: Programs, policies, and social justice*. Rutgers University Press.

Rogers-Ard, R., Knaus, C., Epstein, K., & Mayfield, K. (2012). Racial diversity sounds nice, systems transformation? Not so much: Developing urban teachers of color. *Urban Education, 48*(3), 451–479.

Ronfeldt, M., & Reininger, M. (2012). More or better student teaching. *Teaching and Teacher Education, 28*(8), 1091–1106.

Rosen, J. (2018). *Black students who have one Black teacher more likely to go to college*. Johns Hopkins University. https://hub.jhu.edu/2018/11/12/black-students-black-teachers-college-gap/

Schaeffer, K. (2021). *America's public school teachers are far less racially and ethnically diverse than their students*. Pew Research Center. https://www.pewresearch.org/fact-tank/2021/12/10/americas-public-school-teachers-are-far-less-racially-and-ethnically-diverse-than-their-students/

Sebanc, A., Hernandez, M. D., & Alvarado, M. (2009). Understanding, connection, and identification: Friendship features of bilingual Spanish-English speaking undergraduates. *Journal of Adolescent Research, 24*(2), 194–217.

Sleeter, C. (2001). Preparing teachers for culturally diverse schools: Research and the overwhelming presence of Whiteness. *Journal of Teacher Education, 52*(2), 94–106.

Sleeter, C. (2017). Critical race theory and the Whiteness of teacher education. *Urban Education, 52*(2), 155–169.

Thomas, M. S., Crosby S., & Vanderhaar, J. J. (2019). Trauma-informed practices in schools across two decades: An interdisciplinary review of research. *Review of Research in Education, 43*(1), 422–452.

Tuck, E. (2009). Suspending damage: A letter to communities. *Harvard Educational Review, 79*(3), 409–428.

Tyrone, H., & Rodriguez-Scheel, A. (2017). Culturally relevant pedagogy 20 years later: Progress or pontificating? What have we learned, and where do we go? *Teachers College Record, 119*(1), 1–32.

Ullucci, K., & Battey, D. (2011). Exposing color blindness/grounding color consciousness: Challenges for teacher education. *Urban Education, 46*(6), 1195–1225.

Valenzuela, A. (2016). *Growing critically conscious teachers*. Teachers College Press.

Villages, A. M., & Lucas, T. (2002). *Educating culturally responsive teachers: A coherent approach*. SUNY Press.

Villages, A. M., & Lucas, T. (2007). The culturally responsive teacher. *Educational Leadership, 64*(6), 28–33.

Williams, K., & Davis, B. (2000). *Educating the emerging majority: The role of minority-serving colleges & universities in confronting America's teacher crisis*. Alliance for Equity in Higher Education.

Yin, R. K. (2012). *Applications of case study research*. Sage Publications.

Yosso, T. (2005). Whose culture has capital? A critical race theory discussion of community cultural wealth. *Race, Ethnicity and Education, 8*(1), 69–91.

Zeichner, K. (2010). University-based teacher education: Rethinking the connections between campus courses and field experiences in college- and university-based teacher education. *Journal of Teacher Education, 61*(1–2), 89–99.

Zeichner, K., & Liston, D. (1990). *Teacher education and the social conditions of schooling*. Routledge.

Index

Achinstein, B., 19, 21
Action research, 100–104
Advocacy, 100–104
American Educational Research Journal, 40
Asian American and Native American Pacific Islander Serving Institutions (AANAPISIs), 1, 4, 43
Assaf, L. C., 17

Ball, A. F., 9
Baptiste, P., 58, 59, 60, 93
Battle, J., 17
Bianco, M., 13, 18
BLOCKS Program, 88–92
Buchanan, R., 17
Bullough, R., Jr., 68

California Mini Corps Program (CMC), 73–76, 94–96
California State University, Fresno
   California Mini Corps Program (CMC), 73–76, 94–96
   Rural Residency Program, 77–80, 84–88
Call Me MISTER (CMM), 69–73, 96–97, 103–104
Canrinus, E., 17
Carver-Thomas, D., 12
Central Valley of California
   teaching in, 49–53
Certification exams, 18–19
Chapman, T. K., 10
Clark, C., 68
Cochran-Smith, M., 100
Coherence
   lack in teacher education programs, 16–18

Cohort models, 67–69
   California Mini Corps Program (CMC), 73–76
   Call Me MISTER (CMM), 69–73
The Color of Teaching (Gordon), 9, 21
Communication of success, 108–109
Community analysis, culturally relevant pedagogy as, 58–61
Community Analysis (CA) Project, 58–61
Community engagement, 108
Community service, 96–97
Cree Medicine Wheel, 45–47, 61
Critical pedagogy, 24
Culturally and Linguistically Sustaining Pedagogy (CLSP), 49–50
Culturally competent teachers, 10
Culturally relevant pedagogy (CRP)
   as community analysis, 58–61
   defined, 40–42
   integrate, 105–106
   and MSIs, 42–43
   overview, 38–40
   at Stone Child College, 44–49
Culturally responsive clinical experiences, 18
Culturally sustaining pedagogy, 41
Cultural pluralism, 41
Culture, essentialization of, 15

Darling-Hammond, L., 81
Dinsmore, J., 68
Diversity
   history of, 7–11
Diversity and Teacher Education (Grant & Gibson), 10
Duncheon, J., 11

Edwards, C., 12
Epstein, K., 55
Equality, equity vs., 8
Equity
  equality vs., 8
  racial. See Racial equity
Experiential learning, 17

Faculty care, 64–67
Field trips, 98–100
Freitas, C., 19, 21
Funds of Knowledge, 100

Galman, S., 13
Garza, R., 17
Gasman, M. B., 63, 68
Gay, G., 15
Gibson, M., 10
Gist, C., 13, 18
Goodwin, A. L., 7
Gordon, J., 9, 21–22
Gorski, P., 14
Grant, C., 10
Gresham, A., 9

Hammerness, K., 17
Hansen, J., 68
Hard-to-staff schools
  recruitment and retention of teachers of color in, 19–20
Haynes-Writer, J., 58, 59, 60, 93
Higher education
  access for students of color, 11–12
Hispanic Serving Institutions (HSIs), 1, 4, 43
Historically Black Colleges and Universities (HBCUs), 1, 4, 53
  teacher education at, 43
Holistic faculty care, 64–67
Holmes Program, 68
Home visits, 94–96
Hsieh, B., 13
Husman, J., 80

Inequalities, savage, 11
Inquiry, 100–104

Jackson State University (JSU)
  Call Me MISTER program, 69–73, 96–97, 103–104
    visibility and black role models at, 53–58

K–12 educators
  former, recruitment of, 107
Klette, K., 17
Knaus, C., 55
Kozol, J., 11

Lack of program coherence, 16–18
Ladson-Billings, G., 10, 40–42
Leadership, peer, 67–69
Learning
  experiential, 17
Loteria Card, 50–53
Love of teaching, 109
Lynn, M., 13, 18
Lytle, S., 100

Making Black Scientists (Gasman & Nguyen), 63
Marchitello, M., 43
Martuza, V., 9
Mawhinney, L., 43, 61, 64
Mayfield, K., 55
Milner, H. R., 13
Minority Serving Institutions (MSIs), 1–2, 22, 62–63
  cohort models, 67–69
  culturally relevant pedagogy, 42–43
  faculty and students as family, 63–64
  mentoring at, 64
  overview of, 4–5
  personalized and holistic faculty care, 64–67
  residency model and, 82–84
  types of, 4
Montana School for the Deaf and Blind (MSDB), 98
Moyer, P., 80

Narratives, 23–37
National Council for Accreditation of Teacher Education (NCATE)
  professional development standards, 9

Index 129

New Mexico State University (NMSU), 93
  BLOCKS Program, 88–92
  Community Analysis (CA) Project, 58–61
  Funds of Knowledge, 100
  Tech at Home, 97–98
  Tech Goes Home program, 98
  youth participatory action research, 101
Nguyen, H. T., 13, 63, 68
No Child Left Behind (NCLB) in 2001, 8

Ogawa, R. T., 19, 21
Olson, B., 17

Pang, V., 9, 17
Parekh, G., 14
Parental education, 97–98
Paris, D. D., 41
Park, C., 17
Peer leadership, 67–69
Personalized faculty care, 64–67
Petchauer, E., 19, 43, 61, 64
Pica-Smith, C., 13
Practice shock, 57
Predominantly White Institutions (PWIs), 1, 7, 43
Preparing Teachers for Diverse Schools (Marchitello & Trinidad), 43
Preservice teacher (PST), 18

Racial equity
  in teacher education, 7–11
Racism, 8–9, 13–14
Residency model
  BLOCKS Program, 88–92
  and MSIs, 82–84
  need for, 82
  Rural Residency Program (RRP), 77–80, 84–88
Rogers-Ard, R., 55
Rosenberger, C., 13
Rural Residency Program (RRP), 77–80, 84–88

Savage inequalities, 11
Sexton, D., 19, 21

Sleeter, C., 8, 14, 16
Stone Child College (SCC), 65, 93
  Cree Medicine Wheel, 45–47, 61
  culturally relevant pedagogy at, 44–49
  field trips, 98–100
Students of color
  access to higher education for, 11–12
Studying Diversity in Teacher Education (Ball & Tyson), 9
Supporting Critical Multicultural Teacher Educators (Gorski & Parekh), 14

Teacher education
  at Historically Black Colleges and Universities, 43
  literature on, 10–11
  racial equity in, 7–11
Teacher Education Across Minority-Serving Institutions (Petchauer & Mawhinney), 43
Teacher education programs, 80–82
  curriculum for SCC's, 45–47
  high stakes entry and certification exams, 18–19
  lack of coherence, 16–18
  presence of Whiteness in, 12–16
Teacher preparation program (TPP), 12
Teachers of color, 11, 12, 18, 19
  recruitment and retention in hard-to-staff schools, 19–20
  Teach for Mississippi, 53–54
Teaching English as a second language (TESOL), 24
Teaching profession
  diversify, 105
  respect for, 108
Teaching profession,
  image of, 21
Tech at Home program, 97–98
Tech Goes Home program, 98
Testimonios, 2, 22

Tomorrow's Schools of Education, 69
Tribal Colleges and Universities (TCUs), 1, 4
Trinidad, J., 43
Tyson, C. A., 9

Wenger, K., 68
Wentworth, N., 68

Whiteness
  presence, in teacher education programs, 12–16
White sensibilities, 14

Youth participatory action research (YPAR), 101

Zeichner, K., 81

About the Authors

Alice Ginsberg is a senior research specialist at Rutgers University-New Brunswick. She has over 30 years of experience in educational programming, teaching, and research, specializing in issues of teacher education, higher education, urban education, Minority Serving Institutions, social justice pedagogies, and educational philanthropy. In addition to teaching at the University of Pennsylvania and Rutgers University, Alice is the author or editor of eight books, including *Gender in Urban Education* (Heinemann, 2004), *Gender and Educational Philanthropy* (Palgrave, 2007, with Marybeth Gasman), *The Evolution of American Women's Studies* (Palgrave, 2008), *Embracing Risk in Urban Education* (Rowman and Littlefield, 2012), and *Transgressing Teacher Education* (Rowman and Littlefield, 2022).

Marybeth Gasman is the Samuel DeWitt Proctor Endowed Chair in Education, a distinguished professor, and the associate dean for research in the Graduate School of Education at Rutgers University-New Brunswick. She also serves as the executive director of the Samuel DeWitt Proctor Institute for Leadership, Equity & Justice and the executive director of the Rutgers Center for Minority Serving Institutions. Marybeth is the chair of the Rutgers University, New Brunswick Faculty Council. Prior to joining the faculty at Rutgers, Marybeth was the Judy & Howard Berkowitz Endowed Professor in the Graduate School of Education at the University of Pennsylvania. Her areas of expertise include the history of American higher education, Minority Serving Institutions (with an emphasis on Historically Black Colleges and Universities), racism and diversity, fundraising and philanthropy, and higher education leadership. She is the author or editor of 33 books, including *Educating a Diverse Nation* (Harvard University Press, 2015 with Clif Conrad), *Envisioning Black Colleges* (Johns Hopkins University Press, 2007), *Making Black Scientists* (Harvard University Press, 2019 with Thai-Huy Nguyen), and *Doing the Right Thing: How to End Systemic Racism in Faculty Hiring* (Princeton University, 2022). Marybeth has written over 250 peer-reviewed articles, scholarly essays, and book chapters. She has penned over 450 opinion articles for the nation's newspapers and magazines and is ranked by *Education Week* as one of the most influential education scholars in the nation. Marybeth has raised over $23 million in grant funding to support her research and that of her students, mentees, and MSI partners. She has served on the board of trustees of The College Board as well as Historically Black Colleges—Paul Quinn College, Morris Brown College, and St. Augustine College. She considers her proudest professional accomplishment to be receiving the University of Pennsylvania's Provost Award for Distinguished Ph.D. Teaching and Mentoring, serving as the dissertation chair for over 80 doctoral students since 2000.

Andrés Castro Samayoa is an assistant professor in the Department of Educational Leadership & Higher Education in the Lynch School of Education and Human Development at Boston College. Andrés's work enhances experiences for students of color from under-resourced communities—specifically focusing on Hispanic Serving Institutions. His expertise includes the social history of large-scale datasets in postsecondary education; educational researchers' use of data to explore issues of diversity; and the institutionalization of services for lesbian, gay, bisexual, queer, and transgender students. Previously, Castro Samayoa served as assistant director for assessment at the Penn Center for Minority Serving Institutions. His current projects concentrate on diversifying the teaching profession at the K–12 and postsecondary levels. One of these projects explores the ways Hispanic Serving Institutions diversify faculty in the humanities and social sciences. He earned his bachelor's degree from Harvard University, his master's degree from Cambridge University, and his doctoral degree from the University of Pennsylvania. He is a member of the Association for the Study of Higher Education as well as the American Educational Research Association.